50 GEMS OF

Cheshire

MIKE APPLETON

AMBERLEY

First published 2019

Amberley Publishing
The Hill, Stroud
Gloucestershire, GL5 4EP

www.amberley-books.com

British Library Cataloguing in Publication Data.
A catalogue record for this book is available from the British Library.

ISBN 978 1 4456 8585 4 (paperback)
ISBN 978 1 4456 8586 1 (ebook)

Typesetting by Aura Technology and Software Services, India.

Printed in Great Britain.

Contents

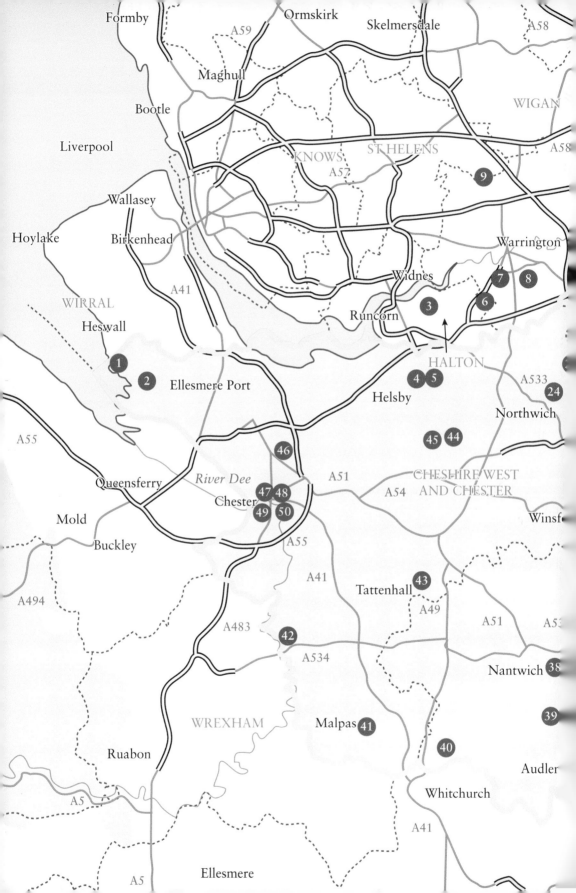

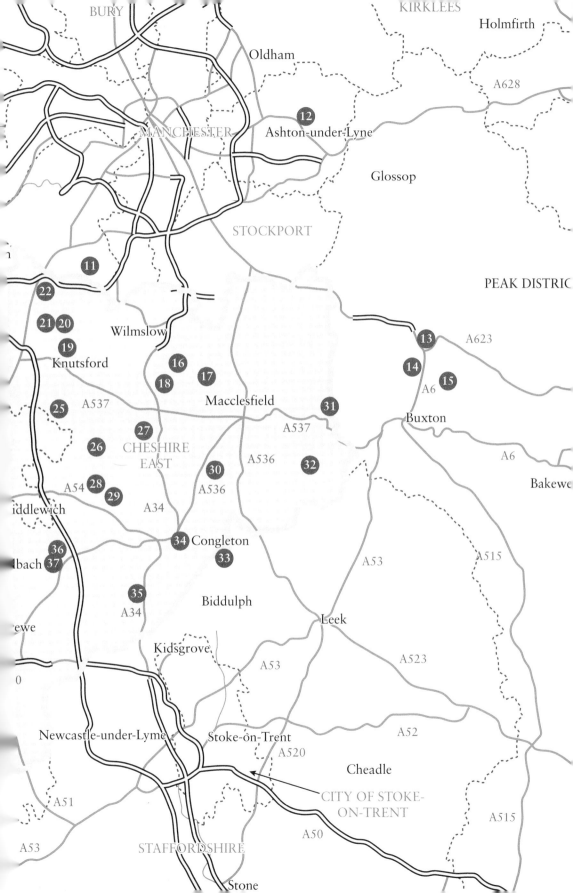

Introduction

Oxford Dictionary states that a gem is 'an outstanding person or thing'.

In my previous books – *50 Gems of the Yorkshire Dales* and *50 Gems of Derbyshire* – these abounded everywhere. Wherever you turned, historical buildings and windswept landscapes were coupled with breathtaking caves, thirst-quenching pubs and other dramatic places. I expected my foray into Cheshire to be similar and compiling a list of must-see attractions would be an easy task. How wrong I was.

For a start, Cheshire is a vast county. The current boundary covers roughly more than 900 square miles but historically was a lot larger. It took in the Wirral and stretched across to Black Hill, which is now in the Peak District and near Yorkshire. It also travelled as far down as Crewe and skirted along the Welsh border.

Then, even though it is relatively flat, it has three distinct 'tops': the aforementioned Black Hill, Shutlingsloe and Shining Tor. Alderley Edge Mines take you underground as does Hack Green Nuclear Bunker. Stalybridge, near Stockport, is as far removed from Ness Botanic Gardens as you can get, as is Newton-le-Willows, part of Merseyside, from the likes of Nantwich and Crewe. Then you could include Flintshire, which is now part of North Wales.

Yet, one thing I have learnt is that great places have a habit of revealing themselves somewhat haphazardly. Instinctively, they come in groups. For instance, the Lovell Quinta Arboretum is a stunning collection of trees in the late Sir Bernard Lovell's garden, the famous physicist and radio astronomer. It is a stone's throw from Jodrell Bank and located in Swettenham, which is a beautiful village in its own right. Delamere Forest has Hatchmere Lake as its neighbour while Parkgate and Ness can be visited in an afternoon.

These places are designed to be visited in clusters, taking time to appreciate why they are gems before you move onto the next. Old Cheshire or new Cheshire, there's a multitude of possibilities and I hope you will enjoy the expanded boundary I have taken my inspiration from.

Naturally, there are several people I owe a debt of gratitude to in producing this work. In no particular order I'd like to thank Tim Baxter, botanist at Ness Botanic Gardens; the landlord at The Castle Hotel in Runcorn and his three boxer dogs; Bernard Platt; Nick Johnson, co-owner of Altrincham Market; the staff at Stalybridge Buffet Bar; Carolyn Latham at Tatton Park for her vast knowledge; Ted Thompson at the Anderton Boat Lift; Lynn Newton at Capesthorne Hall; Rhod Taylor at Lovell Quinta Arboretum for his tour; Frances and Antony Cunningham at the Swettenham Arms; Lucy Siebert at Hack Green Nuclear Bunker; Steve Grenter, heritage & archives lead at Wrexham Council; Will and the team at Chester Zoo; Nick Fry from Chester Cathedral; and Jamie, the barman at the Falcon Inn.

I am indebted to Renuka Russell for her Alderley Edge Mines trip report. She is one of the kindest people I have met in the course of writing my books and, as a fellow caver, was prepared to venture where most wouldn't!

These people made my experience in Cheshire all the more special and I am truly thankful for the passion they displayed for where they live. This book is dedicated to them all and I hope their energy comes through in these pages.

Enjoy the gems, or, as I define them, 'an experience that resonates; those places that capture the imagination, spark further interest or just feel comfortable, rewarding and nourishing'.

Mike Appleton
April 2019

A Note

For clarity, the gems are displayed in four loosely defined 'sections': north-west, north-east, south-west and south-east.

These boundaries are not official and have been drawn using a certain amount of licence from the author. Some of the locations of the gems on the adjoining map are approximations too and therefore within each description are detailed ways of finding it.

As always, I am indebted to the fine folks at the Ordnance Survey. The maps I used in the course of writing this book are Explorer 257, 266, 267, 268 and 276. I also used OL24 and OL1, which cover the Peak District.

North West

1. Parkgate

For everything Cheshire has to offer, the last thing you would expect to find is a coastal resort.

Therefore, it is fitting that a village on the Wirral Peninsula becomes the perfect place to start our tour of the region, because it is just so unexpected.

Parkgate was an important port towards the end of the seventeenth century, serving as a leaving point for Ireland. Originally, ships docked further in stream at Chester but as the River Dee silted, alternative disembarkation points were needed. The first was built at Burton but as the river became less navigable, a location was found just outside the boundary of Neston's hunting park. Parkgate was that 'post' and it became a bustling hub with ships anchored in the main channel – passengers and goods transferred by tender. It retained that status until 1815 before the majority of trade with Ireland passed through Liverpool.

Parkgate is an important salt marsh…

... and has great views.

Parkgate's sands and waters were also notable for their healing powers right up until the 1930s. It is thought that Lady Emma Hamilton bathed here to cure a skin complaint. Nearly ninety years later, the landscape has become a salt marsh, which is a haven for wildlife. The area is managed by the RSPB, who purchased it from British Steel in 1979. Hen Harrier, Merlin, Skylark, Redshanks and Short-Eared Owls all call it home – with even more arriving when tides flush out mammals and insects.

Taking a walk along the Parade is like stepping back in time. The site of the Old Customs House, once a starting point for donkey rides, provides a host of information, while on the opposite side of the road is Mostyn House School from 1855, the Ship pub and places to buy local seafood and the resort's famous ice cream.

Details:
Parkgate is best approached from the A540, via the B5135. Parking can be found at the end of the Parade.

You can find out more at www.rspb.org.uk/reserves-and-events/, searching for Parkgate. News and tide information can be discovered at www.visitparkgate.co.uk.

2. Ness Botanic Gardens

'It's a pretty garden isn't it?' Sometimes the humblest of descriptions sum up what a gem is all about, and this single succinct line does exactly that when talking about Ness Botanic Gardens.

Set across 64 acres, superb design, vivid colour and horticultural instinct come together to create a garden that you simply can't take in during one visit.

It was founded in 1898 by Arthur Kilpin Bulley, a famous socialist and cotton broker. He rarely spent money on material things, preferring to support social causes – he stood as a Women's Suffrage candidate in the 1910 election – but invested heavily in his garden. He also used his wealth to sponsor species collection all over the world as Tim Baxter, botanist at Ness, explains on a tour of the site.

Above and below: The vibrant colours of Ness.

'Bulley was a pioneering plantsman,' he said.

He introduced plants and species to this country but never went on trips himself. He would pay people to do that for him, probably because he had a lot of sense. These expeditions would be undertaken in the most difficult and remote places. He sponsored George Forrest and on one of his first trips the monastery he was staying in was attacked and he was the only westerner that survived. He went back the next year and recollected the species he'd lost.

These were tough people and they would go out for two years at a time to remote regions with big mountains, valleys and rivers.

Bulley effectively started the careers of Forrest, Francis Kingdon-Ward, Reginald Farrer and was one of the first westerners to really commercialise plants. Like any good horticulturalist, he believed the best way to look after any kind of plant was to give it away. If he grew it himself, he could lose it, but someone else could grow it successfully.

He also founded Bees Seeds here which eventually moved to a site at Sealand. The idea wasn't to make money; he wanted to ensure the masses could beautify their garden like he did. It was designed to sell seed cheaply.

Bulley's contribution to horticulture, not just in this country but around the world, is important but he was never really recognised by the Royal Horticultural Society (RHS). I think they didn't like a left-wing socialite being one of the guiding lights of horticulture at the turn of the twentieth century.

Bulley died in 1942 and his garden passed to daughter Lois. Understandably, during the Second World War, little was done on the site and by the time it was given to the University of Liverpool, it wasn't in the best of conditions.

'Gardens are as much about people as the plants, and you can see that reflected if time and care isn't invested,' Tim added.

The garden was first offered to the RHS, but they didn't want it, probably because of political reasons, and the National Trust wouldn't take it because the endowment wasn't large enough. The university was the third choice really and it wasn't until the late 1950s that it became a proper botanic garden once again.

In 1957, Ken Hulme was appointed director and almost the entire structure of the garden is down to him. I suspect that very little of Bulley's garden was left when he had finished. Ken was a director until 1989 and his list of developments is pretty long considering he had very little money and staff. He had time and that made all the difference.

He planted the herb garden which is sadly now gone, the Laburnum arch, rebuilt all the glass houses and established the herbaceous borders. Most of the older trees were planted by him too. He trained at Edinburgh and had lots of contacts. He created the garden for education and the outer areas for science.

My predecessor is Hugh McAllister who is an expert on Rowans, Birches and Ivy. He is very well known in the plant world and like most of us, slightly eccentric. He is a walking dictionary whose forte is taxonomy and the naming of species. What Ken and Hugh did was restart a garden that was more than just a pretty park.

The science was based around having a really interesting plant collection and we have some very important plants here primarily from Western China, continuing Bulley's ethos and legacy. We also have collections from Forrest and Ward too. That is the good thing about a botanic garden. We can study plants here rather than going out into the wild. We have important collections of Birches, Rowans and Alders. I think we have things that many gardens wouldn't have in the rest of the world.

A walk around Ness brings you into contact with all these plants and most are named – Tim says he must produce 1,000 labels a year – so the layperson can have a pretty good idea at what is going on. There's a children's play area, as well as a café and shop, but you'll want to spend time in the gardens, rather than inside.

Some plants thrive at Ness because of the micro-climate. It can be wet in Wales, just a short distance over the Dee Estuary, but relatively dry on the Wirral. It has the same rainfall as the east coast and therefore a similar longer, drier, growing season. It's also quite windy, which keeps fungal diseases and other pests away. The winters are mild and that's good news as anything that likes a humid environment tends to die quite quickly here.

'Bulley liked testing things and didn't seem to worry about failing,' Tim added. 'If something didn't grow, he would try it elsewhere on the site. He laid "monthly beds" which saw things growing and flowering depending on the date. It would have been spectacular, but to be fair he had a 6 acre garden and forty-eight gardeners. We have 64 acres with just seven!'

The extent of work here is mind-blowing. There are thousands of plants in the garden and record keeping is difficult with such a variety of species. Ness used to be famous for rhododendrons too, but they've gradually been lost through the years. However, this has released space for other things to be planted.

'I've been here for ten years and would say I know most of the Rowans on the site,' Tim continued.

I know what has been planted during that time, but as for what is actually here … that's more difficult as our records aren't great. Mr Bulley didn't keep records; he knew what the plants were, so it wasn't an issue. These days we do try to keep tabs on everything but it's a hard task as we are given things and there are lot of historic plants.

We know 90 per cent of our Birches are from the wild and that is unusual for a garden. Most usually grow them, but we try and take them from the wild. We have close to 300 different types of Birch which have been collected from the wild. In all, I would estimate there are 8,000 types of plant in the garden and probably 30,000 in total.

The water garden is a popular place for marriages.

As well as having its own weather station, Ness houses the Brian Moss Aquatic Mesocosm Facility that looks at how small invertebrates react to climate change. There are fifty ponds involved in the research and they are already revealing some important findings.

Then, there's a collection of late-flowering azaleas, which are named after places on the Wirral and a wonderful water garden and terrace where, if you would like to, you can get married.

'Bulley's motto was "welcome friend, welcome stranger, welcome one and all" and I'd like to think we continue that ethos now,' Tim says as we come to the end of the tour. 'He was a very warm person who did what he could to support the local community. That's a rare thing these days. This garden means an awful lot to an awful lot of people and I hope people see that too when they come here.'

Details:
Ness Botanic Gardens is open all-year around with ticket prices depending on the season. It is best approached from the M56 and then the A540, following the brown signs. www.liverpool.ac.uk/ness-gardens/.

3. Halton Castle

While very little of it remains, Halton Castle, and in particular its view over the River Mersey, is well worth visiting allyear round.

According to Historic England, it was established in around 1070 by Hugh Lupus, the Earl of Chester, who gave permission for Nigel, 1st Baron of Halton, to build a motte-and-bailey timber castle on the site.

John of Gaunt upgraded it in the fourteenth century, while in 1457 a new gatehouse was added at a cost of £347, taking seven years to complete. The castle was also used as a prison in 1579 for Catholic recusants and in the mid-seventeenth century it was

Little remains of Halton Castle, but it's dramatic all the same.

The view from Halton Castle.

captured by Sir William Brereton in the Civil War. Under Cromwell, it was partly demolished in 1643.

Access to the ruins is usually restricted to heritage open days but you can explore them by simply popping into the Grade II listed Castle Hotel. This was originally a courthouse, built by Henry Sephton and John Orme, which replaced the gatehouse in 1737 and continued to be in operation until 1908. It's certainly not the most picturesque of pubs but the beer garden is understandably a real draw.

The landlord is more than happy to let you to take your drink and have a look around the castle – and that stunning view – while being accompanied by his three very friendly boxer dogs!

Details:
The Norton Priory Museum Trust manages the castle on behalf of the Duchy of Lancaster and, as stated, visitors are not normally allowed access to the site other than on heritage open days. The Castle Hotel does allow entry, however, provided you buy a drink! www.nortonpriory.org/about/halton-castle/.

4. Frodsham

This wonderful town is a busy little place with its high street and thoroughfare fit to bursting at any time of the week.

Initially, settlement here was on higher ground – still evidenced on Frodsham Hill – and the Domesday Book describes 'Frotesham' as a village held by the Earl of Mercia. By the time the town was founded as a free borough in around 1230 it had moved to lower ground.

Thatched
cottages
in historic
Frodsham.

The Frodsham Heritage Economic Regeneration Scheme, which has posted interpretation boards all around the town, notes that Ranulph de Blundaville, the Norman Earl of Chester, established the town and 'burgage plots of one acre were established along what is now known as Main Street … people were freed from their agricultural dues and encouraged to earn their living from trade'. This move was key and would later see the town host a flourishing market, re-established in 1661, and a port that took full advantage of its location near the mouth of the River Weaver at the point it joins the River Mersey.

What Frodsham does well is mix its heritage with the everyday. Buildings of note don simple blue plaques and the town's symbol of a honeybee is evident throughout, homage to Revd Williams Charles Cotton, a former parish vicar and expert on beekeeping.

The Bears Paw pub was built in 1632 and used to be called the Lion's Paw. In the eighteenth century it even contained a post office. Further down the high street, to the left, are some beautiful thatched cottages, and across the road are timber buildings from the seventeenth century. The library was built in 1837 but was a Wesleyan Association Tabernacle Chapel before it became a place for books a century later, and the Queens Head Hotel is one of the oldest in the town. In 1799, it housed a cotton factory!

Details:
Frodsham can be found on the A56 and is best approached from either junction 12 or 14 of the M56.

5. The Sandstone Trail

Running for 34 miles, this trail takes in some of the best countryside in Cheshire on an unbroken route that stretches from Frodsham to Whitchurch in north Shropshire. It follows the wooded sandstone ridge that arcs from the top of the Cheshire Plain to the bottom.

The traditional start of the 34-mile Sandstone Trail.

Strenuous in parts, but not many, it's classed as a middle-distance trail and is used by around 250,000 walkers per year. Not all walk the full route – and it can be completed in seven different sections, ranging from 3.5 to 6 miles, or, if you fancy a good hike, in two or three larger chunks.

It was first conceived by Cheshire County Council's Countryside and Recreation Department in the early 1970s, but it wasn't officially designated until 1974. Originally, it spanned just 16 miles – cutting a track from Delamere to Duckington – but its popularity saw it lengthened. Beacon Hill, near Frodsham, and Grindley Brook Locks in the south were soon added, and in the late 1990s it was extended slightly further to take in the current start and end points and give people better transport links.

This isn't a Pennine Way where navigation is key; it's waymarked throughout and it is worth heading to the excellent www.sandstonetrail.co.uk to find out more.

Features include six prehistoric hillforts, Woodhouse, located within the first few miles of the trail from Frodsham, Delamere Forest (see gem 45), a hidden glacial meltwater gorge called Urchin's Kitchen, Beeston Castle (gem 43), the National Trust's Bulkeley Hill, Bickerton Hill and Whitchurch itself.

It's geologically important as you're following a ridge that has Triassic sandstone that is likely to be more than 225 million years old. It was formed when sand and sediment were compressed, creating the conditions for iron oxide and other minerals to form. These help 'cement' the stone and give it its distinctive red colouring that creates such an iconic landscape.

Details:

The Sandstone Trail begins in Frodsham (next to the Bears Paw) and ends at Jubilee Park in Whitchurch.

It is waymarked by a 'black boot print containing the letter "S" on a yellow background' and further details can be found at www.sandstonetrail.co.uk.

6. Daresbury

It feels fairly nondescript as you park in a lay-by but a few hundred metres up a path is the birthplace of one of the most famous writers in the world.

Charles Lutwidge Dodgson, or Lewis Carroll to give him his pen name, was born outside the village of Daresbury in 1832, on what is now a fairly lush oasis of calm away from the busy conurbations nearby. He spent eleven years of his life in the area, but his parsonage home was ravaged by fire and is now just etched by an outline.

The site is managed by the National Trust – the Woodland Trust's Lewis Carroll Centenary Wood nearby – and there is a well that is covered by iron workings and a dormouse design that symbolises his life. There's plenty of spots to sit and take in nature too while the light filters through the trees and it's easy to ponder if such a scene could have inspired his *Alice's Adventures in Wonderland*.

Lewis did return to the village when he was twenty-eight years old to take pictures of the places he knew as a child and five years later the first of Alice's adventures were published.

You can discover more about Carroll's life in the Lewis Carroll Centre back in the village. It's located in conjunction the All Saints Church, itself a historical gem. In the twelfth century it was a chapel for Norton Priory and then a pink sandstone parish church was built in 1550.

Details:
Daresbury is just off junction 11 of the M56. It is sensible to park at the centre/church because parking in the village is difficult.

Lewis' birthplace is a forty-five-minute walk from the village centre but there is parking in a lay-by near the site. Simply follow the brown signs from Daresbury. www.lewiscarrollcentre.org.uk.

What is left of Lewis Carroll's birthplace.

7. Walton Hall and Gardens

Walton Hall more than deserves its place in our list not just because of the variety of things on offer but the fact it is all family friendly.

Formal gardens, pitch and putt, bowls and a children's zoo can be visited alongside many other events for people of all ages.

The flowers in particular are spectacular and impressive for a council-run venture. No doubt officials at Warrington have their budgets spread thinly to maintain such a standard of gardens has to be applauded. Some of the displays are akin to those at Tatton and are a must see in spring. Rhododendron, bluebells, tulips and azalea come into their own at this time while the bedding plants are superb in summer.

The hall itself isn't open for visitors. It is Grade II listed and was built in 1836 for Sir Gilbert Greenall, a local brewer (Greenall Whitley & Co. Brewery was famous throughout the region) who would later become MP for Warrington. His son, Gilbert Greenall, 1st Baron of Daresbury, inherited the property in 1894 and lived there until he died in 1938.

Warrington Council took ownership of the property and gardens in 1941.

Details:
Entry to Walton Hall and Gardens is free. Parking is £3 from Monday to Friday or £4 over the weekend and bank holidays. www.warrington.gov.uk/info/201129/walton_hall_and_gardens.

Right, below and opposite: Walton is impeccable and colourful at every turn.

8. Lumb Brook Valley

Sometimes gems appear by word of mouth, recommendation or just pure luck. After researching autumnal places to visit, up popped an article from *Wanderlust* about great regions to visit as the leaves turn. Its article 'Go for gold: Where to see Britain's best autumn colours' listed eight spots and Lumb Brook was one of them.

The 'valley', roughly 26 acres in size, is a series of interconnected woodlands that are distinctive and full of character. Fords Rough begins the Brook and is an area of Ancient Semi-Natural Woodland. It features oak, ash, wild cherry, alder, rowan, birch, holly, hazel, hawthorn and elder alongside wood anemone, bluebells, lesser celandine as well as mosses, liverworts and ferns. Next is the Dingle – another Ancient Semi-Natural Woodland – then Julia's Wood and Long Wood.

Considering there is a lot of development in Appleton, it's testament to the Woodland Trust that Lumb Brook is as good as it is. Their management is very important and no doubt future work to encourage the ecosystem to flourish is planned.

Importantly, for the casual visitor, this gem is right next to where you can park. You're in it straight from the car and that makes it one of the most accessible gems in Cheshire!

Details:
The best area to explore is from Dingle Lane in Appleton, Warrington, WA4 3HR. Park in the lay-by on the left as the road rises and you can explore the valley on either side. www.woodlandtrust.org.uk/visiting-woods/wood/4543/lumb-brook-valley/.

Wanderlust indeed! The magazine chose Lumb Brook as a place to visit in autumn, and we agree!

9. Newton-le-Willows

A settlement in Newton, or Neweton, was recorded in the Domesday Book with the additional 'In Makerfield' added in the thirteenth and fourteenth centuries to make it discernible from others. Newton-le-Willows followed much later, in 1939, and it became part of St Helens in the 1970s.

Its position as a focal point for industry and innovation is as strong as any in the country. In the nineteenth century, it became the world's first railway town as it took full advantage of being on the route of the world's first passenger railway from Liverpool to Manchester. In fact, this goes over the Sankey Canal, the country's first canal, on the Sankey Viaduct.

On the flip side, in 1830, William Huskisson MP was killed at Parkside when he was run down by Stephenson's Rocket on the opening day of its operation.

The nearby Vulcan Foundry was opened in 1831, one of the world's foremost locomotive manufacturers, and Vulcan village remains a conservation area. Newton also grew as it became a hub for coal mining and other industries.

Then you have the fact that the fields near Newton were the scene for the defeat of the Highlanders (1648) during the Second English Civil War, and there was a castle just a few hundred metres from the town's centre.

Sankey Valley Park. Walk along the country's first canal. (Bernard Platt)

Newton has a superb heritage trail. (Bernard Platt)

While much of Newton is now quite urban, it does retain its heritage charm. Its original centre, on the A49, has Georgian buildings, and comes under protective status in terms of development. Its high street has a number of really good independent shops and some great pubs too. A heritage trail links all these together in a fascinating 6-mile circular walk.

Probably the best part of the town is St Peter's Church, which is on a natural bend at the eastern part of the High Street. Despite being on a main road, it is a place of remarkable solace. While the existing building is more modern, a church has stood on this site since at least 1242 according to officials from St Peter's. However, the Newton Heritage Trail indicates that the 'earliest reliable reference to a chapel in Newton occurs in 1284 when Sir Robert Banastre was granted a chantry in his chapel'.

The original St Peter's was rebuilt in 1683–84, consecrated in 1735, and enlarged in 1819 and 1835. It was then completely rebuilt between 1892 and 1898.

Backing on to the church's grounds is Willow Park and Newton Lake. The park was originally part of the Legh family estate, and the lake created in 1853 by Thomas Legh, the then lord of the manor. It was built to provide a recreation area for the gentry.

To the left of the church and up Castle Hill is a mound of earth that is the surviving part of a motte-and-bailey castle dating from the early part of Norman Britain.

Details:
Newton-le-Willows is accessible from either the M6 (J23) or M62 (J10).

For details on the Heritage Trail head to www.newtonheritagetrail.com.

North East

10. Lymm

The origin of 'Lymm' comes from the Celtic phrase meaning 'place of running water'. It is thought an ancient stream ran through its centre, hence the name, and these days the Bridgewater Canal passes close by.

Mentioned in the Domesday Book as 'Lime', it was once a parish of the Old Bucklow Hundred. It is a charming village with boutique shops and picturesque places to watch the world go by as well as the superb Lymm Dam, which is close to 500 metres from the centre.

It was built in 1824 as engineers constructed an earth dam to cross a pool in the valley below St Mary's Church. They did this to create a road link between Warrington and Stockport, which is now the present-day A56. That pool soon became a lake and was part of Lymm Hall estate, which owned much of the village.

The Bridgewater Canal.

The dam is a real tourist attraction and a place of great eco-diversity that includes the Bongs, an area of Ancient Semi-Natural Woodland at its southern end.

Back in the village centre, it's worth pausing at Lymm Cross and the stocks in front. The cross was restored in 1897 but built in the mid-seventeenth century. It has a stone ball and ornate weathervane that is likely to date from the same era.

Details:
Lymm can be found on the A56 and there is parking available near the Bridgewater Canal.

11. Altrincham Market

Markets used to be a focal point both socially and economically in many towns across the country.

The cacophony of stallholders advertising their wares would illuminate a street, centre or indoor venue and people would seek out a bargain and get their fresh daily produce from the sellers they trusted.

I edited the *Market Trader* newspaper for a few years in the mid-2000s and can remember the smells, sounds and banter that these 'salt-of-the-earth' places would create. They were hubs for folk and gave an area character even though the shopping mix was already changing.

Sadly, thriving markets like this are now few and far between. Habits have changed, big retailers offer a simpler retail opportunity and many markets missed the boat as times moved on.

However, what can be seen from the success of continental street markets, particularly at Christmas, is that people do want something different from the norm – a real, authentic and unique experience. Altrincham Market certainly provides this and is a foodie's paradise!

Its origins stretch as far back as 1290 when Edward I granted a royal charter allowing the town to hold a weekly event. Such was its success, people flocked to

An historic market, totally transformed. (Claire Harrison Photography – www.claireharrison.com)

the area to work and live and the town expanded. To cope with demand, the market began running three times a week: on Tuesdays, Fridays and Saturdays. That growth continued until the mid 1990s before shopping habits changed and it declined.

Left with no real choice, Trafford Council put it up for tender in 2014 and that's when Nick Johnson and his team stepped in.

'Altrincham Market, like the town centre around it, had been in decline for decades but we knew it had the potential to be so much more,' he explained.

> Working as deputy chief executive of Urban Splash, a Manchester-based property developer renowned for turning large disused buildings around the UK into luxury apartments and workspaces, I'd spent the best part of twenty-five years changing other people's places yet Altrincham, where I lived, was failing. I wanted to change that.
>
> We had the vision of creating a modern, European-style food market at the heart of the town and after six months of refurbishments, it opened in September 2014. Three years on from the relaunch of Altrincham Market, we led a similar transformation of Mackie Mayor, a former meat market in the Ancoats area of Manchester, built in 1858.
>
> Over the last five years, Altrincham market has helped bring the town centre back from a 25 per cent vacancy rate in 2014 to 10 per cent today. The market now turns over more than £5 million a year.

As a popular town in a really affluent area that borders Hale, Wilmslow and beyond, the demise of Altrincham was quite stark. Projects, including a new residential and retail offering, are still on a drawing board to bring regeneration, but it's likely the biggest impact to the town's economy was the building of the Trafford Centre in 1998 and the easy links to Manchester via the tram system.

To create a modern, thriving market, and regain the town's status as a real destination, is really impressive – and it's been done without gimmicks. Yes, you can sit in a communal food hall, watch your food be prepared and chat to your fellow shoppers, but it's all quality and well worth the money. Offerings include wood-fired pizza, flat iron steak, craft beers and wines, award-winning pies, chocolate and great coffee to name but a few.

'By hand picking talented independent businesses and not investing in vanity real estate we helped provide a reason for people to visit the town again,' Nick added.

The success of the market area has acted as a catalyst to further Altrincham's 'foodie' reputation and its revived restaurant scene has meant footfall to the town has increased year on year as the market's pull spread to the rest of the town centre.

On average, visits to UK town centres are down 17 per cent over the past decade and more than one in ten shops have stood empty for at least a year. However, Altrincham has bucked the trend and I think most would agree that the market has played a huge part in this.

We looked to create a 'total' experience – shopping, eating, drinking and entertainment with each component part delivered by hand-picked independent businesses from across the north-west of England. All our vendors are passionate and independent.

He continued:

The market is tapping into people wanting something different, something better. Today's consumers want an experience that's worth leaving the comfort of their front rooms for – and the only way to do it is to bring in quality goods that you can't buy online and reward customers with an experience that you don't get sat at home.

We also give people a chance. Unlike the high street where occupants face leases and business rates that are payable regardless of their trading performance, here we charge the new businesses we take on a percentage of their turnover. It means less risk for them and no need for failing businesses to wait for a lease to expire before quitting and leaving a void.

Ultimately though, the market's success is down to our traders, the kitchens and the people we have got in them, all being incredibly good at what they do.

No gem can afford to rest on its laurels, but it seems to me that Altrincham Market has the best of both worlds – great food and produce in a great environment. It's also

The food on offer is superb. (Claire Harrison Photography - www. claireharrison.com)

eco-conscious – the majority of fruit and veg comes from a 35-mile radius – and they have drastically cut down on non-recyclable plastic waste.

Nick says that another area of Cheshire could get the same treatment shortly: Macclesfield.

'Expansion-wise, the success of Alty Market is capable of being repeated, as Mackie Mayor has shown,' he continued. 'We've recently lodged plans – alongside Manchester architect Buttress, whom we worked on the Mackie Mayor project on – for a food hall at Macclesfield's Picturedrome.'

'Macclesfield seems like a natural next step to us.'

Details:
The market can be found at Altrincham Market House, No. 26 Market Street, Altrincham, Greater Manchester, WA14 1PF. It is signposted and there is car parking available.

The market can become really busy, but it is well worth the wait.

12. Stalybridge Buffet Bar

For people who like nostalgia, a good pint and a quirky dining experience, look no further!

Dating from 1885, the Stalybridge Buffet Bar is one of very few remaining 'pubs' of its type in the country. This Victorian station buffet bar has retained all its original features including black marble-topped bar and is packed with railway history and other artefacts. Then, you have a selection of real ales, gins and many others that are well kept, changed often and are award winning.

Did I mention it's also right on the platform at Stalybridge too? Leave the car at home – you'll need to as the bar demands a long stay.

The Buffet Bar dates from 1885.

It has a great bar.

My visit came just before Christmas and it was pretty busy with people taking a break before their next train came along, trippers like myself, those dining and a number working away at their PCs.

On the left is a conservatory that was opened in 2009 after a £50,000 project saw the original 123-year-old structure replaced. It's a relaxing place to have a drink and doesn't look like a fairly new addition. In fact, it's tastefully done with lovely stained-glass windows and memorabilia, much like the rest of the bar, which was destined for demolition in 1994.

The station itself began life in 1845 but was replaced by the existing building in 1885 because of demand. At that time, the 'buffet' was a conservatory, bar and kitchen. On the right is a small corridor and another beautiful room before it opens out into a larger dining area with an ornate ceiling. This was the first-class ladies waiting room and it's a complete contrast to the bar area. That ceiling seems a lot higher and therefore it is a lot more 'airy' than other areas.

The bar is the place to be though, and once you've done sampling the beer there is a fantastic array of food on offer. This includes pies, sausage rolls and scotch eggs that can be taken away as you board your train. Not everyone's cup of tea of course, but rustic, home-made and keeping in with the surroundings. There's also an extensive menu too if you're not in the mood for snacking.

Stalybridge Buffet Bar is also part of the Trans Pennine Real Ale Trail, which takes in eight great pubs – all on a train!

Details:
Stalybridge Buffet Bar can be around at Stalybridge railway station on Rassbottom Street, SK15 1RF. It is open from 11 a.m. on Tuesday to Saturday and noon on Sunday and Monday. www.beerhouses.co.uk/pub/stalybridge-buffet-bar/.

13. The Gritstone Trail

If you're looking for a slightly strenuous trail that takes in parts of Cheshire and beyond then the Gritstone Trail provides such a challenge.

It's a 35-mile route, officially recognised on 6 August 1978, that starts in Disley and ends in Kidsgrove in Staffordshire, climbing 5,276 feet in the process and topping out at Sponds Hill (1,342 feet). It follows the Gritstone edge that passes through the county and gives great views of the neighbouring Peak District and the Cheshire Plain.

Lyme Park, Sponds Hill, Tegg's Nose Country Park, Croker Hill and Mow Cop are all visited and there are many other routes that can be taken including the Ladybrook Interest Trail Walk at Lyme, the Staffordshire Way and South Cheshire Way at Mow Cop. For that reason, the route can be walked in around three days, but it is possible to tag on an extra day or two.

Starting at Disley, the trail takes you south to Lyme Park (gem 14) before emerging onto moorland and near to the Bow Stones, thought to be the remains of Anglo-Saxon crosses. Further on, you pass 'White Nancy,' a landmark built in 1820 to commemorate the Battle of Waterloo.

Tegg's Nose is an impressive country park to the south-east of Macclesfield and its summit is a great place to see the gritstone you have been following up close. Next you pass Bottoms Reservoir and Tegg's Nose Reservoir and then Meg Lane End, which was apparently home to highwaymen who robbed travellers on these routes!

The final third of the trail sees you pass through some more spectacular scenery including Edge Hill, which is part of the Congleton Edge. The Old Man of Mow is a

Mow Cop Castle in Biddulph. (Paul Stringer/Shutterstock)

gritstone pillar that stands at more than 20 metres and the next landmark is the folly of Mow Cop, built in 1754 by Squire Wilbraham to improve the view from Rode Hall. Mow Cop itself is seen as the home of Primitive Methodism. The Wesleyan Memorial Church was built in 1862 on the site of the first open-air meeting that took place in May 1807.

At Kidsgrove station it's worth continuing along the Trent & Mersey Canal to see the entrance to Harecastle Tunnel, itself stretching more than 1.5 miles to Tunstall in Stoke-on-Trent.

Details:
The route is well waymarked with a black boot mark and a yellow G, but it is recommended that you use Ordnance Survey Explorer map 268 and the Explorer OL1 Dark Peak map.

Explorer map OL24 is also useful.

14. Lyme Park

Managing large estates is something that the National Trust does really well and in Lyme Park they have one of the best in Cheshire.

The Grade I listed house, which is the largest in the county, has around 15 acres of gardens and a deer park of close to 1,360 acres. It was granted to Sir Thomas Danyers in 1346 and passed to the Leghs of Lyme just over forty years later. The National Trust took on the estate in 1946 and, as well as developing it into a complete heritage attraction, have completed some significant environmental work. The Lime Avenue ponds, for example, were restored in 2017.

The grounds are something the estate prides itself on and are worth the entrance fee alone. To the west of the house is a former millpond and sunken Dutch garden, with flower beds and a fountain. There are rose gardens too.

Probably the most photographed part of Lyme Park is 'The Cage', which is on a prominent hill as you approach the house. It was formerly a hunting tower and

Deer in the grounds of Lyme Park. (National Trust Images/ Arnhel de Serra)

gatehouse before becoming a park keeper's house and a prisoners' lock-up. An original structure was constructed in around 1580 before it was taken down in 1734 and rebuilt three years later. The first floor was the main room with an oak ceiling that featured a carved rosette in the centre.

Back at the house it is clear why people flock to visit Lyme. It dates from the late sixteenth century with modifications made by Giacomo Leoni and the Platt family of masons. They completed the courtyard plan in around 1725 before Lewis Wyatt made alterations from 1814. The gardens were fairly late additions in the nineteenth and twentieth centuries.

Inside, it has a stunning array of artefacts including tapestries and collars belonging to the family's mastiff dogs! It's also possible to visit the house's wardrobe department to try on some of the costumes of the era.

Probably its finest piece is the Sarum Missal, the only surviving copy printed by William Caxton in Paris in 1487. It contains the liturgy for Mass and was in the family's possession from the early sixteenth century before it was bought by the trust in 2008.

They say that, 'Sir Piers Legh V, both a knight and a priest, bought the book and most probably used it to officiate services. It then lay forgotten and dormant after the Reformation until it was rediscovered by Peter Legh XII. He repaired the book in the eighteenth century only for it to disappear again. In the 1870s it was then given pride of place in Lyme's Library until leaving with the family in 1946'.

Once it returned to Lyme, the library was completely redecorated for what the trust considers is the most important printed book it has.

Although handwritten copies of the Mass were fairly common, this was the first to be printed by Caxton alongside Parisian printer Guillame Maynyal. The Missal here is unique as it also shows verses crossed out as requested by Henry VIII during the Reformation. However, the lines are faint so the passages could still be read, and they have also been rewritten at the back, indicating how important the Catholic faith was to the Legh family.

Details:
Lyme Park can be found at Disley, Stockport, Cheshire, SK12 2NX.

www.nationaltrust.org.uk/lyme provides a detailed description of opening times, what's on offer and entrance prices.

The Grand Staircase. (National Trust Images/ Chris Lacey)

15. Black Hill

Reaching 1,909 feet, Black Hill isn't a particularly majestic 'mountain' or somewhere that would be high on many peak bagger's lists, but it retains a certain charm as well as being a real oddity.

The views on the way up to the summit are amazing on a clear day and getting to that point is relatively straightforward – from the A635 and along the well-paved Pennine Way, if you're inclined to take that route.

Its location makes it important too. Black Hill is the highest point in the historic county of Cheshire, but now effectively sits on the border between the borough of Kirklees in West Yorkshire and High Peak in Derbyshire. Yes, it's a Cheshire hill, in the Peak District near West Yorkshire!

It got its 'bleak' name because it was once covered in deep black bogs; exposed peat stripped back due to 150 years of pollution and wild fires.

Paddy Dillon, one of the authorities on the Pennine Way and a fellow Outdoor Writers and Photographers Guild member, says that the hill was 'once so over-trodden

The view on the Pennine Way.

At the top of Black Hill.

that it was often impossible to reach the trig point which stood on a firm island known as Soldiers Lump'. This was where Ordnance Survey experts set up camp while surveying the land.

The difference between that description and the present day couldn't be more contrasting as significant conservation efforts have taken place.

Remedial work started on the 46-hectare site in 2003, aided by the Heritage Lottery Fund, before the Moors for the Future MoorLIFE project came to the fore. They spread 50 million sphagnum fragments on the moorland to reintroduce sphagnum moss, a key peat-building moss. They also planted bog cotton and bilberry, and these are evident as you reach the summit.

Details:
Park in the lay-by on the A635 where the Pennine Way meets the road. Follow the well-paved route towards Black Hill, crossing Dean Clough, which can be difficult to ford in poor weather. The walk there and back on the same path is around 3.5 miles.

16. Alderley Edge Mines

These mines are owned by the National Trust and leased to Derbyshire Caving Club (DCC), who have played a vital role in restoring the inner workings of this historical site.

Access is via guided tour through the DCC, or on open days for a fee, as young and old are invited to discover how copper was mined here. It isn't an arduous trip, lasting around an hour, and a helmet and lamp is provided.

Fellow caver Renuka Russell was fortunate enough to join Robert Stevenson and Gary Beech from the DCC on a more in-depth visit alongside Bri Edmonds and Bill Hanley.

She recounts their trip by explaining how copper began to be extracted here.

'Unlike the Victorian lead mines of Derbyshire, this mine is huge, a testament to how rich it once was in copper,' she says.

Extraction in the West Mine, which was the first port of call on my trip, dates back to 1857. It was undertaken by the Alderley Edge Mining Company Limited and by 1860 more than a thousand tons of ore was being extracted every month.

Removing it was painstakingly hard work and often dangerous. Miners would work by candlelight and use hammers and chisels to bore 'shot holes' into the sandstone. These would then be half-filled with gunpowder together with a fuse. The hole was then blocked with red clay, the fuse lit, and the explosion would bring down the ore.

The miners would break it up and would get $7d$ per ton and a further $5d$ per ton for taking it to the crusher and filling the acid tanks with the crushed copper ore.

Some of the more experienced miners came from as far afield as Cornwall and on our visit, we saw examples of their signatory rock shelving, a particular technique used in the mines in that region.

Wooden trucks on rails would then take the ore to the haulage incline where they would be pulled up using ropes or chains attached to a steam engine on the surface. You can still see the marks of the trucks deeply grooved into the walls in some sections. There are also rotting wooden sleepers and evidence of where the old rails were laid.

The crushed copper ore was placed in leaching tanks on the surface. There were sixteen of these, each capable of handling 9 tons of ore. Hydrochloric acid was

Below left and right: The spectacular colours of mineralisation in the Engine Vein. (Renuka Russell)

added to the ore and the resulting highly acidic liquid would drip down through the false bottom of the tank. Underneath, scrap iron was piled in and this caused a chemical reaction with the acid. The resulting precipitate contained both copper and iron and was sold at different prices according to the percentage of copper.

The West Mine first closed in 1878 but reopened twice as the price of copper rose before it was finally abandoned in 1919.

Renuka continues:

We accessed the mine via a shaft, climbing down an iron ladder and it wasn't long before we came to a massive chamber more than 15 metres wide, 12 to 18 metres high and several hundred metres long.

Guided by Gary, the tour lasted around six hours – much further than the open days – and we undertook a very detailed exploration into the chambers and passageways, as well as some optional flat out crawls and tight squeezes.

There were a fair few ladders to be climbed too, taking us into the deeper levels and in some places the miners had carved steps into the rocks. Many of the smaller passageways had been hand-picked, which look beautiful, but I'm sure that would have been an extremely laborious way of working.

We also came across the blacksmiths where the miners would bring their tools in for repair and saw where the furnace would have been. Around the mine are many 'tally marks' – these are short diagonal strokes made with a pick axe. They were used by the miners when they dug a barren patch or made alterations to existing passages. As with so many mines there is extensive graffiti on the walls and roof too, usually the names of the individual miners and the managers and much of this dates back to the 1850s.

We also found a section that was dug out for use as an air-raid shelter during the Second World War. These passageways are a bit superfluous given that the rest of the mine has an enormous capacity and is well protected underground!

Bri was the geologist of our group and after he explained how they extracted the copper he pointed out secondary mineralisation on the walls, particularly the beautiful green malachite. We also saw the 'Green River', an outstanding display of malachite and we were mindful not to step over the tape as conservation is of utmost importance in these historic mines. Likewise, other artefacts such as drill bits, gunpowder measuring vessels, crowbars, shovels, old newspaper cuttings, bottles, cans, clay pipes and cigarette packets are left in situ and protected as an integral part of the mine's heritage.

Renuka next talks about the 'The Shaft of a Thousand Planks' – stemples placed one above the other all the way up the shaft.

'Originally it would have gone to surface and a brazier of coal been suspended over the top of the shaft in order to draw out the pollution,' she added.

Nuggets of coal can still be found scattered around the bottom of the shaft and the rusted remains of a thick chain has been laid to one side. This would have been attached to an anchor point on the surface and then dropped down the shaft. It was designed not to touch the floor but be suspended about 10 feet above it. At the end of his shift a worker would climb onto a platform, reach for

The Green River.
(Renuka Russell)

the chain and attach the leather loop that was at the end of the chain around his ankle. He would then proceed to climb the shaft on the wooden rungs. Should he accidentally slip and fall, this chain would stop him hitting the bottom!

Rob explained that the mine workers weren't given money in return for their labour but issued tokens instead. These could be spent at the Alderley Edge shop on candles and food. Likewise, beer could be purchased in the same manner from the local pub. It was a type of debt bondage as the workers could not choose where to spend their tokens and the local prices were undoubtedly inflated.

Towards the end of the trip we came across a large pile of stones and Gary informed us it was referred to as 'the Monday morning pile'. He went on to describe how the miners worked 6 days a week but had Sunday's off to attend church. Afterwards, they would be found in the pub drinking themselves into oblivion. Monday morning, they would stagger into work, two sheets to the wind or nursing bad headaches, and definitely not in a fit state to do anything other than the simplest tasks!

The Monday Morning Pile would have been put together by the workers, during the week, a bit at a time, and it served the sole purpose of making it look like they were working hard come Monday morning. In actual fact they were merely chucking the ore rubble into the tubs to be carted out of the mine!

While the focal point of the workings was in the West Mine, there was also the Wood and Engine Vein on the site. The former was probably referred to as eastern mine and it began operations a few years after the West Mine, as did Engine Vein.

Renuka adds:

At the surface of Engine Vein there is evidence of Bronze Age pits dating from around 1900 BC. That is a very early example of copper extraction using stone hammers. In Roman times, a shaft was sunk into the mine and in 1995 a hoard of Roman coins was discovered by DCC. In Blue Shaft, there are examples of secondary mineralisation including the almost unreal deep blue of azurite.

It is an amazing set of mines and I'd encourage anyone to take a trip through them on one of DCC's open days. You won't be disappointed!

Details:

Visits to the Alderley Edge Mines have to be arranged with a DCC member but there are open days during the year. For details visit www.derbyscc.org.uk.

Many thanks to Renuka Russell for the trip report here alongside Gary Beech, Robert Stevenson, Bri Edmonds, Bill Hanley and all at Derbyshire Caving Club. Renuka recommends reading *The Alderley Edge Mines* by Chris J. Carlon and Nigel J. Dibben (Altrincham: John Sherratt & Son Ltd, 2012).

17. Prestbury

Prestbury is one of the prettiest villages in Cheshire with a history stretching back to Anglo-Saxon times.

Originally known as Preosta, which means 'dwelling of the priests', it wasn't recorded in the Domesday Book but that doesn't mean it didn't exist before the end of the eleventh century.

It is thought that its lack of notation was due to it being a small dwelling or church rather than part of something bigger, or, of course, the information hadn't been supplied on time. Yet, there is plenty of evidence that it did play a significant role in the area.

Two Saxon churches are thought to have been present on the site of St Peter's Church before it was built and there is also an eleventh- or twelfth-century Norman chapel in the churchyard. There are remains of a Saxon cross too.

The current St Peter's is impressive, and the churchyard is a bastion of peace away from the busy road it fronts. It is Grade I listed, with construction beginning in 1220. What cements this as an important site of worship is the fact that when the new building began to take shape, it took place separately from the Norman chapel. This seems to indicate local contributors wanted something special in the village, or the Norman chapel wasn't suitable enough for them to incorporate the new structure around. The chapel itself was rebuilt in 1747 by Sir William Meredith of Henbury so that generations of his family could be buried there.

The Legh Arms in historic Prestbury.

The Norman chapel dates from the eleventh or twelfth century.

Over the next three centuries the church was enlarged, and a tower erected before it was extensively restored and extended by Sir Gilbert Scott in 1877.

The Saxon cross was discovered in the masonry of the chancel in the nineteenth century. It is now on display in the churchyard and indicates that worship on this site was occurring during the ninth or tenth centuries. The churchyard also contains a sundial from 1672.

Elsewhere in the village are a number of buildings that are historical. One such example is directly across the road from St Peter's: the Priests House, a black and white timber-framed building from 1448. The Legh Arms, known locally as the Black Boy, is worth calling in to as is the Ye Olde Admiral Rodney, a seventeenth-century coaching inn. It features low ceilings and panelled walls as well as great guest ales!

Details:
Prestbury can be found off the B5087 and A538, around 3.5 miles from Macclesfield.

18. Nether Alderley Mill

I have to profess I have a particular affection for Nether Alderley Mill. As a primary school pupil, I made several field trips to the site to see how wheat was milled and got the chance to see some of the machinery in action. As a kid it was great to leave the confines of the classroom and experience something different.

Nether Alderley Mill still held that joy the last time I visited. Access is by guided tour only on Thursdays, Saturdays and Sundays from April to September and the person taking me through its inner workings once again managed to spark my interest.

There's evidence of a mill here as far back as 1391. Documents indicate it was a watermill, but it isn't clear if that means there was a mill at Nether Alderley or at this place in particular. In the late sixteenth century it was rebuilt and some of that work can be seen in the existing basement.

The National Trust, who manage the site, say that in 1746 it was 'enlarged to its current size of layout' and it 'used salvaged materials from the earlier building – stonework and roof timbers all show evidence of having been re-used'.

The nineteenth century saw a new upper waterwheel and cast-iron mechanism installed as well as a new lower waterwheel and tunnels cut underneath to remove water more easily. A new cast-iron hurst frame and gearing was also added, and between

The fully restored medieval building of Nether Alderley Mill. (National Trust Images/John Millar)

The mechanism of the fully restored medieval Nether Alderley Mill. (National Trust Images/John Millar)

2008 and 2012 the 'sagging' roof was restored using specialist stonemasons, millwrights, carpenters and joiners. Parts of the mill were also replaced including the teeth on the gear wheels. Visitors can see it in action on the tour that takes around an hour.

Details:
Nether Alderley Mill can be found on Congleton Road, Nether Alderley, Macclesfield, Cheshire, SK10 4TW. Parking is limited on site. Access is by guided tour only on Thursdays, Saturdays and Sundays from April to September.

Prices start from £5.45 for adults (£6 gift aid) with further details at www.nationaltrust.org.uk/nether-alderley-mill.

19. Knutsford

Knutsford is a busy hub that is best visited either via public transport or by getting there very early. Parking and traffic are an issue but don't let that put you off what is one of Cheshire's real jewels.

Knutsford was recorded in the Domesday Book as 'Cunetesford', linking it to King Canute, who was king of England in 1016–35. Local folklore says that he blessed a wedding and forded the River Lily, although this could have been another water course in the area. In 1292, a charter was granted to William de Tabley by Edward I to allow a court, market and fair to be established and, apparently, it was once a famous cockfighting centre as well as the inspiration for Elizabeth Gaskell's *Cranford*.

It's worth beginning your visit at the Knutsford Heritage Centre, which is located in a seventeenth-century timber-framed building – a former blacksmiths – on King Street. It has plenty of information to whet your appetite and give you an overview of the town and its history. There's also the possibility to enjoy guided walks during the summer. King Street is the lower part of the town – including an entrance to Tatton Park (gem 20) – with Princess Street the 'top'.

The Angel is a cracking pub on King Street – a former posting house – as is the Rose & Crown while The Old Sessions House on Princess Street is also worth a visit.

Elsewhere is the Gaskell Memorial Tower, which was built in 1907 by Richard Harding Watt. He said that the author's books had given so much joy that the town should acknowledge what she did. She is buried in the Grade I listed Brook Street Unitarian Chapel, the oldest place of worship in Knutsford. Watt was a glove manufacturer who liked Italy, and you can see that influence in many of the buildings in the town. Knutsford has an eclectic mix of structures and buildings, but they somehow work.

On May Day the town comes alive with a parade and the May Queen is announced. The streets are also decorated with coloured sands.

Details:
Knutsford is easily accessible from the M6 at junction 19.

20. Tatton Park

Tatton is one of the most renowned and iconic parks in the world.

It is a honeypot destination in an already busy area of the county and a short visit isn't really possible unless you just fancy walking around the grounds and watching Tatton's deer – which has its merits of course. The parkland covers 2,000 acres and includes woodlands, meres and farmland, half of which are accessible to the public. It was landscaped by Humphrey Repton in the late eighteenth century, although deer have roamed the area since 1290. Rare breed Hebridean and Soay sheep have also been a feature here since 1887 and were reintroduced in the 1930s.

This environment is key to Tatton's overall appeal to visitors and a team of rangers make sure it is as eco-diverse as possible. The meres and Dog Wood are dedicated SSSI and RAMSAR sites with work carried out in the latter to improve biodiversity. Those rangers look after 500 acres of woodland, which house several rare species alongside important wildlife.

Equally important are Tatton's Gardens (which we will take a glimpse at in the next gem) and Tatton Dale farm. At its height it fed family, guests and staff at the mansion, alongside the produce grown in the garden. It needed to perform well as the Egertons, who owned the estate, liked entertaining and throwing opulent dinners, particularly in the Victorian era.

It's a great place for families to walk around and at the right time of the year it's possible to see many little piglets in the farm's nursery. It is a rare breeds farm and

The mansion at Tatton overlooking the gardens.

accredited by the Rare Breeds Survival Trust, just one of seventeen farm parks with that accolade in the country.

It is worth buying the Totally Tatton Ticket so you can access the mansion, gardens and farm for a special price. All the attractions don't have to be visited in one day on this ticket either.

Above, below and opposite: Plenty of gems lie within the mansion. (Tatton Park)

The Old Hall is Tudor and located where the former Tatton village used to stand. It is a Scheduled Ancient Monument, built as a manor house by either the Stanley family or Sir Richard Brereton at the turn of the fifteenth century. By 1598, it had grown via a two-storey wing added by Sir Thomas Egerton, Lord Chancellor of England, who then owned the estate. It then became used as worker cottages and tours highlight the life and times of those living in them.

The hub of the park is naturally the mansion house, the first stage of which was built in 1791. Before then, the Egerton family came into ownership of the park in 1598 when it was bought by Thomas Egerton from his half-sister Dorothy Brereton. It wasn't until close to 120 years later that John Egerton realised its importance and established a permanent residence on the estate.

His son, Samuel Egerton, commissioned architect Samuel Wyatt to produce designs for a new neoclassical mansion house. He passed away in 1791 before the first stage was completed and it was Wilbraham Egerton who furnished and purchased many of the paintings and artefacts that are still on display. From there, an upper floor was added to the family area in the 1860s and a family entrance hall completed in 1884, at the same time as electricity was installed. This was a point of interest for the people who would stay at the mansion. Electricity via generator was a real indicator of Earl Wilbraham Egerton's enthusiasm for the very latest technology and having such a system in place was a status symbol to those who visited. It was the wow factor! Tatton Park had a great social scene and the Egertons provided it.

Innovations also include a heated towel rail in the Chintz Bedroom and a heated tin bath in the Silk Dressing Room. Here, the bath would be filled with hot water and kept warm by red-hot charcoal in a firebox at the bottom end of the bath.

Alan de Tatton inherited the estate when Earl Egerton passed away and he refurbished the mansion and developed the Rose and Japanese Gardens. Then came

Maurice, the last Lord Egerton, who left the mansion and gardens to the National Trust on his death in 1958. He was quite a character who travelled extensively as well as being a pioneer aviator, photographer, filmmaker and motorist. He spent a lot of time on his Kenyan estate and was a compulsive collector, some of which can be seen in the Maurice Egerton Exhibition Room.

The items reflect his vast travelling experience with a model kayak from the Yukon being on display alongside a number of musical instruments from Africa and beyond and a meteorite! The library contains at least 8,000 books with a further 4,000 elsewhere in the house. The artworks are staggering and include Van Dyck, Poussin, Chardin, Carraci and Guercino. Then you have Gillow's of Lancaster furniture and fine ceramics too.

The special mixture of house, gardens, farm, park, shopping and dining make Tatton a real gem. A simple chapter cannot do it justice...

Details:
Tatton Park is well signposted from junction 19 of the M6 and 7 of the M56. It is recommended that WA16 6SG is used for satnav while it is also possible to access the park from the lower part of King Street in Knutsford.

Each 'attraction' – house, gardens and farm – has its own collective ticket as well as single access. Note there is an additional cost for car parking.

For prices and opening times visit www.tattonpark.org.uk.

21. Tatton's Gardens

At 50 acres it's easy to lose track of time in Tatton's Gardens...

The Japanese Garden is phenomenal. You can see pineapples being grown in the glasshouses, spend longer than expected in the Fernery and pause to admire the view outside the house – all within a few minutes' walk of each other.

Each part of the garden has a particular mood and hidden gems that you will certainly miss on a first visit, while realising the intricacy and brilliance of the people who have tendered them before and still do today.

It is thought they were first 'planted' in 1715 with each owner of the estate subsequently leaving their own distinctive fingerprint. Famous architects Joseph Paxton and Lewis Wyatt were vital in designing the conservatories as the Egerton family reacted to the trends of the time. Maurice also played his part, adding rhododendrons and azaleas, which are a real highlight of the gardens, particularly when they come into colour in late spring and early summer.

One of the first places to visit is the Walled Gardens. This is where a lot of vegetables and fruit for the mansion would have been grown. It still is utilising the techniques of the past. On the top of one of the walls you will notice ornate pots, but these aren't there for decoration. Ever the innovator, these are chimney pots for the heated walls. Waste from the garden was fired in the wall cavities to help ripen fruit and lit again in the spring to help protect them from frost.

Amazing topiary.

The orchards are beautiful and produce fruit that hails from the Edwardian period as well as distinctive Cheshire-based varieties. These, as well as pears and plums, are available in the shop when in season.

Just to the left of the entrance you have a unique pinery. This was restored in 2007 and, according to Tatton, 'is possibly the only genuine, rebuilt example of a Pinery Vinery in existence in Britain'. It was originally designed by Samuel Wyatt in 1774 as the pineapple was seen as a real status symbol in Edwardian times. It would cost a small fortune to cultivate one, as the pinery would have to be kept at a temperature of around 21°C by hot air flues warmed from fires or, in later years, hot water pipes – and they only fruit every third year! People would even hire them to put on their tables such were their wonder. Tatton's pineapples were famous and would win awards, costing the modern-day equivalent of around £5,000.

The glasshouses were built in the mid-1700s and still grow all manner of fruits such as peaches, grapes and figs. Others include varying types of orchid and it is thought that the garden historically had twenty orchid houses.

My personal favourite is the Fernery and its extensive collection from New Zealand and Australia. It was designed in the late 1850s by Joseph Paxton and is a sensory overload when visited on a rainy day. Once inside, it's tropical and the greenery is really enlightening, as is the small waterfall at the far end.

There's plenty of differing plants and trees as you continue your walk through the gardens, but another true highlight is the Japanese Garden. Unless you land on a guided tour, it can only be seen from its perimeter but that isn't a bad thing as you get a nice overview of the design.

It is inspired by Alan de Tatton's visit to the Anglo-Japanese Exhibition at the White City in London in 1910. It's a tea garden with a particular focus on harmony with nature. It also has a mound capped off with white stones to represent the sacred Mount Fuji. It's best visited in spring when the cherry blossom is doing its thing, but a slight mist on the lake made it magical when I was there in early autumn.

Other places that have to be seen are the arboretum, which contains several hundred plants – some collected abroad by the family; the Rose Garden, established in 1913 for Lady Egerton, the wife of Alan; and Charlotte's Lawn, which was designed by Lewis Wyatt to match the mansion's library furnishings in 1814.

Above: The gardens are vast.

Below: The Japanese Garden.

Kids will love the maze and the African hut built during the war to remind Maurice of his estate in Kenya, which was unvisitable.

Details:
For prices and opening times visit www.tattonpark.org.uk.

22. Rostherne Mere

Cheshire's meres are important internationally because of their habitat and wildlife, with Rostherne in particular being one of the most renowned. It sits in a National Nature Reserve that covers more than 150 hectares and attracts several thousand birds in winter.

Wildfowl including pochard, mallard, teal, pintail and shoveler are regular visitors, while ruddy duck, gadwall and goosander often visit too. The reedbeds house warblers and bitten and the surrounding woods have woodpeckers, owls, sparrowhawks and kestrels. Otters have recently returned and there are colonies of harvest mouse unseen in the area alongside several important species of butterflies.

Therefore – and I say this tongue in cheek – it seems a shame that you can't actually get up close and personal to the mere itself, but that's fully understandable considering its importance.

Pleasingly, there are plenty of opportunities to view it from afar. You can explore its western boundary and a circular path leads around the southern part. There are also four woodlands in the NNR, but only one is accessible at Wood Bongs. There is a small path and you can park up in Rostherne village to access.

To birdwatch you need to contact the Cheshire and Wirral Ornithological Society, who will grant use of the AW Boyd Memorial Observatory for a nominal fee. There's also the chance to join several guided walks.

Details:
Rostherne Mere is north of Rostherne village between Altrincham and Knutsford off the A556.

For details on the AW Boyd Memorial Observatory visit www.cawos.org/rosthernemere.

It may only be viewed from a distance, but the mere is a serene sight.

23. Great Budworth

There's no doubt that Great Budworth is the most attractive and picturesque village in Cheshire. Nothing comes close. From its pretty church and great pub to chocolate-box terraces, there simply isn't anything like it in the county.

For centuries it was part of the Arley Hall estate, and it only left its control in 1948. Before then, Rowland Egerton-Warburton had the church restored and worked with architects such as John Douglas to look at the rest of the village.

He remodelled the George & Dragon, which was originally a three-bay Georgian inn. He added tall chimneys, mullioned windows and a turret and it still houses many original features including a 1722 stone plaque and oak and post fence with a verse from Warburton. Douglas also restored Goldmine House and its attached Rose Cottage.

The Grade I perpendicular St Mary and All Saints Church is very impressive and open all-year round. It was built in sandstone and is breathtaking internally. The nave ceiling dates from the first quarter of the sixteenth century while in the Warburton Chapel are five oak stalls likely to be from the thirteenth century. In the sanctuary are two Jacobean chairs. Elsewhere, memorials form a real feature and include one to historian Sir Peter Leicester as well as the Warburtons.

Back in the village, there are some houses and cottages that make the perfect postcard, Dene Cottages were built in 1867 and on the 'high street' are four Grade II buildings constructed in the early eighteenth century.

Nearby, there's a library in a postbox too!

Details:
Great Budworth is best approached off junction 19 of the M6. For those driving, CW9 6HF will take you to the village centre.

Beautiful terraced house near the church.

The fantastic George & Dragon.

24. Anderton Boat Lift

When someone feels a personal connection to a place it shows in every facet of their emotion.

Parking up at Anderton Boat Lift and taking the short walk to the Trent & Mersey Canal, I paused at the hulk of the lift to take a few snaps before heading into the visitor centre. It was a quiet morning but there were a few people in the cafe, so I stepped out onto a viewing platform to see the structure in its glory. A chap stood next to me and I asked him if I could get down to the riverside to take some pictures. He told me I could and then asked me if I wanted to know anything else. I said yes and he duly beckoned me into the café.

Ted, as his name badge suggested, told me he was a volunteer for the lift and talked me through its history.

'It was completed in July 1875 mainly because of salt,' he explained.

This area had exploration of rock salt to the tune of about 400,000 million tonnes. Along the canal were a lot of saltworks and they would load up the narrow boats, offload through hand carts and then put it down a gantry into a chute which would go into boats on the River Weaver below.

Boaters would line their vessel with tarpaulins so the water wouldn't affect the salt. Sometimes they brought in coal and shipped out salt so they would have to be cleaned in-between. Clay would come here from other areas to be unloaded too and then sent on to Stoke-on-Trent for the potteries. It was a laborious process.

The Weaver Navigation Trustees asked their chief engineer, Edward Leader Williams, to see if anything could be done to relieve all these boats and make the process quicker and more efficient. First of all, he thought about putting locks in, but because they would have been used by so many boats the Canal would have dried up. If there had been a river at the top and canal at the bottom it would have worked.

Edward got in touch with Edwin Clark, who had designed a hydraulic ship lift at the Royal Victoria Dock in London, to see if it could work here - and it did at first.

The first lift was 60 feet high, 85 feet long and 49 feet wide, while the aqueduct was 165 feet long. It was designed to lift boats that would be sat in a container of water known as a caisson. Two caissons would counter balance each other and by draining a little water from the lowest nearly all of the work would be done by the heavier one travelling down, lowering it on a hydraulic ram.

The upward caisson would stop short of the required position and a steam engine would then do the rest. Each tank weighed 91 tons when empty and 252 tons when flooded. They were big enough for two narrowboats or one barge.

'It worked really well but was altered to electric in 1908 because the salt in the water was causing mechanical issues,' Ted continued.

It was eating away at the metal. Each tank was counterbalanced and attached by wire ropes. Two electric motors would help move the lifts and it had seventy-two gears, the largest ones doing the majority of the work.

In 1983, British Waterways put scaffolding around the lift to undertake some maintenance but when they shot-blasted it, they found it completely unsafe. A year later, a lady wrote to our MP about what was happening as there had been a lack of progress. There was a meeting with the Waterways chairman, and he admitted they didn't have the money to complete the work. Spurred on, that lady started a campaign to raise the funds and awareness, and it continued for the best part of eighteen years.

The new lift opened in 2002, cost £7 million and was fully hydraulic. Oil travels from one ram into another to move the boats but it still looks like it did in 1904. The lift is open to private boat passages every day from late March until early November. It is then open on Monday and Wednesday mornings and Friday afternoons during the winter season, closing for maintenance every January. The visitor centre is open every day and weekends during winter.

I've been here as a volunteer in some way or another for thirty-four years and that lady was my wife. It is a real personal project for me, and she passed away more than ten years ago.

Ted's a great storyteller and leaving this bit of news to the end brought home to me how attached he is to Anderton. Christine Thompson will long be a part of this area; she started the process of what is here today – a real gem in ensuring the lift is viable for generations to come.

'I enjoy coming here, it beats being inside watching TV anyway!' I'd agree with that.

Anderton is the 'Cathedral of the Canals' and Ted's personal story ensures it is his church. It is an amphitheatre of engineering and the whole experience makes it ideal for a family day out. It is also possible to enjoy a boat trip on the lift too and there is a play area for the kids.

Attached are Northwich community woodlands too and a walk to Ashton's and Neuman's Flashes and back will take around ninety minutes.

Details:

The Anderton Boat Lift, Lift Lane, Northwich, Cheshire, CW9 6FW, is free to visit but there is a cost for parking. For details and opening times visit www.canalrivertrust.org.uk/anderton.

View of the top of the Anderton Boat Lift.

A feat of engineering.

South East

25. Capesthorne Hall

Built between 1719 and 1732 and set in 100 acres of fantastic parkland, Capesthorne Hall is another of Cheshire's great historic houses.

Open to the public on Sundays, Mondays and bank holidays until the end of October, it's a stunning place in a stunning location.

Capesthorne was held by the family of the same name until 1386 when it was passed to the Wards. A column in the grounds marks where it stood. In 1719, John Ward asked William Smith to design a new house and chapel close by, Francis Smith taking on that role after his older brother died. The estate then passed to the Davenport family with Davies Davenport's grandson improving and extending it further. Further development took place between 1837 and 1839 as Edward Davies Davenport had the 'lateral wings' joined to the main part of the house. The orangery was also replaced with a conservatory designed by Joseph Paxton.

Capesthorne is still in the ownership of the Bromley-Davenport family and has been open to the public since 1951. You can see the family's collection of art, sculptures, tapestries and furniture from all around the world.

In the grounds are a number of gems. The family chapel was designed by William Smith and remodelled in 1887, while there is also an icehouse dating from the late eighteenth or early nineteenth century and a summer house that used to be the bell turret of the chapel. The site also features signs of a medieval village.

A historical hall in a stunning setting: Capesthorne Hall. (Capesthorne Hall)

The saloon.
(Chris Hanley
Photography)

The landscaped park brings visitors in from far and wide and it's clear to see why. Through eighteenth-century Italian Milanese gates, which are themselves a real feature, there is parkland, formal gardens and lakes as well as an arboretum containing maple and cherry trees. It's an ideal wedding spot and the hall caters for that perfectly.

Details:
Capesthorne can be found at Siddington, Macclesfield, Cheshire, SK11 9JY. Entry prices start at £10 for adults for the hall, gardens and chapel and opening times and other information can be found at www.capesthorne.com.

26. St Oswald's at Lower Peover

Pretty village churches are a common occurrence in Cheshire, but none take the breath away as much as St Oswald's.

From its hidden location and black and white frame, it is a real gem. It claims to be the oldest arcaded wooden church in Europe but that is a mere footnote in its splendour.

There has been a church on this site since 1269 when Richard Grosvenor, who resided at Hulme Hall alongside local parishioners, built a chapel of ease at Lower Peover. The idea was to save the congregation the journey to Great Budworth, close to 6 miles away.

A sign inside the church says materials used were those at hand – 'oak and mud and reeds and the building followed no style of architecture'. The original building comprised the nave and its narrow aisles while in 1322 a disused font from the Norton Priory was added. In 1464, the aisles were widened, and a chantry built. The sandstone tower was constructed in 1582.

The oldest arcaded wooden church in Europe.

From there, the Shakerley chapel was added in the south-east corner (1610) and fourteen years later, a Holford chapel to the north was built, taking over the vestry. In 1851, the single-span roof was replaced by a triple gable structure and another refurbishment carried out under architect Anthony Salvin. That roofing had to be restored in 1947 because of dry rot in the timber 'and some worm and deathwatch beetle destruction in other parts'.

Inside, the history of the church is brought into full focus. The wooden arches supporting the roof are a work of art and are home to several birds. The box pews date from 1620 and three bear the crests of three families that endowed to the church. The aforementioned Shakerley's emblem depicts a hare and wheatsheaf, while there are also those dedicated to the Cholmondeleys and Leycesters.

Those pews are fascinating as many retain their original half doors. The top part of the door opens so you can get in while the bottom is fixed to hold in the rushes and straw that were used to keep the congregation's feet warm. These would be renewed each year in a 'Rushbearing' ceremony. The screens, pulpit, choir stalls and lectern also date from the seventeenth century.

There are breadshelves dated 1720 and 1739, which were introduced to accommodate the bread charities left by parish priest Richard Comberbach and his wife – and each Sunday loaves are still left on them.

There's also a bog oak chest that is likely older than the church itself. It's in the Shakerley chapel and was used to keep records, robes and other important items safe. Tradition says that 'if a girl wished to be a farmer's wife, she should be able to lift the chest lid with one arm!' Apparently, this came from the fact that such a spouse had to be strong enough to lift the Cheshire cheeses made in the area. Up to you if you believe that one...

St Oswald's hasn't shied away from its history and throughout the church there is information on what you can see as well as a multitude of materials to buy. There's is a touch of humour too. 'The Glass is all modern' one reads, 'though it is recorded that there was much ancient glass, Cromwellian vandalism has seen to it that none remains'.

Back outside, the Lych Gate takes its name from the Saxon word for corpse. Bodies would be carried to this entrance point in a shroud for the first part of the funeral service to begin. The present gate was built between 1877 and 1911 under Revd Arthur Guest.

The interior
of St Oswald's.

Details:
The church can be found at The Cobbles, Lower Peover, Knutsford, Cheshire, WA16
9PZ. Information on Lower Peover itself can be found at www.lower-peover.co.uk.

27. Jodrell Bank

The Discovery Centre at Jodrell Bank is a place where you can spend a very
informative and enlightening day finding out how this remarkable observatory
became the forefront of astronomical exploration.

It was established in 1945 when Sir Bernard Lovell came to the University of
Manchester to observe cosmic rays following his work on radar during the Second
World War.

The Lovell
Radio
Telescope.
(Andrew
Barker/
Shutterstock)

Since then, it has gone on to research and observe meteors and pulsars for example, as well as being a pioneer in tracking probes in the space age.

Anyone who has been to Jodrell Bank will notice the huge Lovell Telescope. When it was built in 1957 it was the world's largest dish radio telescope at 250 feet in diameter and completely steerable. It was operational in time for the Soviet Union's Sputnik 1 launch and that was useful as it was the only telescope able to track it. It also used to follow probes from the USA as well as using radar to measure distance between planets and other observations.

You can walk around the telescope and marvel at its sheer size – some 3,200 tons. Work on renovating it began in 1999 after the surface was beginning to corrode. It cost around £2 million and a new galvanised surface was added as well as a new drive system so it could be pointed easily. That work was completed by 2003 and a new visitor experience announced in 2018.

The observatory is part of the Jodrell Bank Centre for Astrophysics that is under the guise of the University of Manchester.

Details:
Jodrell Bank can be found just off the A535 between Chelford and Holmes Chapel. It is best to come off at junction 18 of the M6. For details and prices: www.jodrellbank.net.

28. Swettenham

Swettenham is an attractive village with the historic Swettenham Arms at its forefront.

A former nunnery, the inn was used to provide accommodation for mourners awaiting funerals at the thirteenth-century St Peter's Church. Bodies were taken for their final service via an underground tunnel the next day.

The pub is a superb place to while away the hours, with a lavender garden to the right providing a great backdrop for a drink and weddings too. To the left is the Lovell Quinta Arboretum (gem 29).

It's perhaps unsurprising that a pub of this age would have a good tale to tell, and according to its owners there have been some ghostly sightings over the years. The website reads,

On 15th November 2005 a customer was enjoying a meal in the dining room. During the meal, a ghostly apparition appeared at the fireplace.

The ghost appeared to be the figure of a nun dressed in black. She spoke to the customer and said, 'My name is Sarah'. She revealed that she was 35-years-old and seemed very sad in her demeanour. She was floating on stairs. The customer was quite agitated about the experience and left the pub very quickly, leaving her husband wondering what had happened to cause the upset.

It turns out the ghost had been seen on previous occasions, but whether you will see it again is a matter of chance – or the strength of your beverage I expect.

Above and below: St Peter's Church.

Across the car park is St Peter's Church, the first part of which was built in around 1260. It has a timber frame in the chancel that dates from 1304. The tower was built in 1721. Further restorations took place in 1935 and the 1960s. The yew trees in its environs are a pretty addition and are likely to come from well before the seventeenth century when they were recorded in the church minutes.

A fine country pub!

Details:
Swettenham is best visited using CW12 2LF as a reference. It is around 5 miles from Holmes Chapel, just off the A54.

The Swettenham Arms website is www.swettenhamarms.co.uk.

29. Lovell Quinta Arboretum

Sir Bernard Lovell created this fantastic arboretum in the grounds of the house he bought in 1948. His vision was to collect a variety of trees and shrubs from around the world, based on the four volumes of W. J. Bean's *Trees and Shrubs Hardy in the British Isles* and establish them in this quiet part of Cheshire.

It was very much a personal project – he was meticulous in keeping records, hand-drawn plans and a card index for each plant – and was at the heart of developing it as the years progressed.

As an astronomy pioneer, that level of detail is more than reflected in his arboretum and his home village, from the creation of the reflection pond to the avenues and areas that symbolised major events in his life.

In 1996, the site passed into the watch of the Cheshire Wildlife Trust and is now with the Tatton Garden Society and the capable hands of Rhoderic Taylor, the curator.

He looks after close to 2,400 plants, some of which are 'champion' trees, and others of international significance and importance. This is an amazing site with a varied and interesting collection.

We met on an autumnal day at the gates of the arboretum, which can be found to the left of the Swettenham Arms. There is an honesty box in a prominent position, with a suggested entry fee of £2.50 per person, but to be honest, the walk is worth a lot more.

Rhod began by telling me how he has more or less 'carte blanche' to use his expertise in arboriculture to continue Sir Bernard's work and curate the site to ensure its species flourish and provide seasonal interest. He started as a lecturer at Reaseheath College and that academic mind is more than evident. Rhod reels off the names of nearly every plant we come across and says of the 800 different species he has in the arboretum, he probably knows around 600. It's the encyclopaedic knowledge that makes this place a real gem because without it, there's no way it can look as good as it does.

He also talked about how some areas within the site have altered over the years. The gales of 2016 had a positive impact in allowing some space to be opened up and different plants introduced. There's stunning snakebark maples, handkerchief trees, ornamental birches and paeonies, while the puddled clay lake was created in 1955–65, filling naturally over the decade.

'I run the site with volunteers,' he said,

and I've been here for twenty years. There's no full-time staff but I certainly feel like I'm here full time. There's lot of different species and some of them are different to identify because they have grown so tall. We try different plants to see how they will grow and are surprised at how well they succeed. We have plants that shouldn't really grow in Cheshire as it is too mild, but they have managed to establish themselves.

I really enjoy what I do and I'm here a few times a week to meet people, manage it and keep it reasonable. How I do that is largely up to me, but I do try and keep to Sir Bernard's original vision. There is an awful lot of work to do with regards to record keeping, communication and label cutting as well as felling and replanting.

When Sir Bernard was alive, he would create a little card for each species he planted. To try and get into his office to see this index was like trying to get into the Bank of England's vaults. Before he died, he gave me access to it as well as his diaries, historical records and plans for the arboretum. That opened our eyes to what was here and has helped create the records we have today.

Such evidence is seen by the labels on each species. It is a staggering amount of work and effort for such a small team and one that should be applauded. Rhod's enthusiasm for his work is important too. Without him, this arboretum would be a shadow of what it is. He takes each tour like it is his first, with a few jokes thrown in as well.

'I put in my own plants,' he continued,

ones I think will work here and ones that are good for the public interest. I go around nurseries and if the purchases are within budget and work then it is

good for this site. We are great for Snowdrops too; they look stunning when they come through.

The key is to have a succession of age classes, so the arboretum keeps going. If we lose one plant, then there is another of the same species ready to succeed it. We have around sixty different species of Oak, forty of Ash, and sixty of Pine. Our Ash and Pine are recognised national collections. Some of the conifers here have been grown from seed by Sir Bernard.

Rhod showed me the western part of the garden first, the hebe collection, which is maintained by the Hebe Society, the remaining eucalyptus trees, which survived two harsh winters in a row, and a beautiful metasequoia 'Gold Rush'.

We also saw the avenues and the crown lifting that has been undertaken to open them up. The Golden Avenue is stunning and stretches from the lake to the end of the arboretum. Then there is an avenue of limes to commemorate Sir Bernard's lectures at the BBC and another that recognises his knighthood. The Crab Apple Avenue is particularly impressive as well. There are sixteen different types here and the fruits are colour rich. Then there is the 'Great Avenue', which had additional trees planted in 1985 by local schoolchildren. The oaks are outstanding too and it's fair to say you'll be surprised when you see them. They don't look like traditional oak trees for sure!

There is one, a daimio oak, that was presented to the arboretum by British plantsman Roy Lancaster, who obtained the seed from the Ming Tombs in China.

That pioneering work is important throughout the arboretum; Rhod explained they were part of a project in conjunction with the Royal Botanic Gardens in

One of the avenues.

A crab apple tree in the Crab Apple Avenue.

Edinburgh that saw seeds from an endangered conifer propagated here with the plan to then take them back to the Himalayas.

As we returned to the Swettenham Arms, we continued to talk about the arboretum in the autumn sun over a coffee. We were joined by Frances and Antony Cunningham from the pub, too, as we mulled over the world.

It's clear Rhod loves what he does, spending time in the outside ensuring one man's legacy continues for the next generation – with his own slant.

And you know what? £2.50 isn't enough for this experience.

Details:
The Lovell Quinta Arboretum can be found at Swettenham Lane, Swettenham village, near Congleton, Cheshire, CW12 2LF. Parking is available at the Swettenham Arms and suggested entry price via an honesty box is £2.50. www.lovellquintaar boretum.co.uk.

30. Gawsworth

You only have to see the picture below here to understand what a beautiful village Gawsworth is.

It's peaceful, tranquil and its church is flanked by two pools, making it the most idyllic venue for a place of worship.

Then, you have Gawsworth Hall, built in 1480 and the former home of Mary Flitton, maid of honour to Elizabeth I and the 'dark lady' of Shakespeare's sonnets. It is open for visitors from May to mid-September, with the equally as impressive Gawsworth New Hall and Gawsworth Old Rectory nearby.

Gawsworth was listed in the Domesday Book as 'Govesurde' with its extensive woodland and enclosures for oxen. These days it is the old hall where most visitors head to and it's understandable considering its black and white frame, paintings, furniture, sculptures and pleasure garden. However, it was the framing of the church that impressed me most about this village. The scene is unforgettable.

A chapel stood on this site in the thirteenth century but the existing church, dedicated to St James, dates from the fifteenth. The nave is from around 1430 while internally there are plenty of historical features including an eight-sided font from the sixteenth century and four tombs of members of the Fitton family.

In the churchyard, the two eighteenth-century gates are Grade II listed and there is a sandstone cross base that is likely to have been from the late fifteenth or early sixteenth century.

Details:
Gawsworth is around 3 miles from Macclesfield along the A536. For opening times and prices for Gawsworth Hall visit www.gawsworthhall.com.

Gawsworth – what a location!

31. Shining Tor

This 1,834-foot hill is the highest point in the Cheshire, although technically now in the White Peak area of the Peak District.

It's best approached from Errwood Reservoir in the Goyt Valley where you can enjoy a relatively straightforward but hilly walk along Cats Tor. The views take in Shutlingsloe (gem 32) as well as Winter Hill and sometimes Snowdon.

A simpler route to the summit is from the Cat & Fiddle pub or alternatively you can park at the Pym Chair car park, which is less than 2 miles from Errwood Reservoir.

From here, you head back to the T-junction you will have turned down and head left. There is then a path on the opposite side of the road after 50 yards. This will take you to Oldgate Nick, Cats Tor and eventually to Shining Tor. It's about 4 miles there and back and it is signposted.

From Shining Tor, you can continue down the hill and then throw a left to visit Errwood Reservoir, which adds roughly another 2 miles to the route. From here you can walk the western side of the reservoir and take the road back up to your car if you so wish or tie in a walk that crosses Windgather Rocks.

Details:
Pym Chair car park is roughly at SK10 5XL or use SK17 6GJ and follow the road up.

The view from the top of Shining Tor. (Helen Hotson/Shutterstock)

32. Shutlingsloe

Cheshire's Matterhorn has a distinctive and appealing profile that makes it a very popular walk, steep in places, and obviously well photographed.

It is near Wildboarclough and that is the perfect place to start if you're looking for a shortish route to the summit. It's a small village that has a great pub – the Crag Inn – ideal for a stop after your walk. It was built as a farm in 1629 but was converted in 1825 and it still has many original features.

You simply take the steep lane to Banktop and Shutlingsloe Farm and then use the path to reach the top. There is a relatively easy scramble to reach the 1,659-foot summit.

An alternative, and probably more impressive bimble, is from Macclesfield Forest. The path from Trentabank Reservoir, itself a really nice place to visit, crosses Highmoor Brook before the hill in all its profile comes into view. You then take the right fork around a third of a mile outside the forest boundary.

The third highest peak in the county, its name is said to derive from the old English 'Scyttel's hlaw'.

Details:

As via the above walk, the easiest route is from Wildboarclough (SK11 0BD), which can be found off the A54. There and back is under 2 miles while from Macclesfield Forest (SK11 0NS) it is around 3 miles to the summit.

A group walking up Shutlingsloe. (Moonchild69/Shutterstock)

33. The Bridestones

Very little of this Neolithic burial chamber may remain but there is certainly enough here to gain an understanding of how grandiose it would have been.

It was originally 110 metres long and around 11 wide and contained three separate compartments, one of which survives today. It also had a forecourt that would have been surrounded by a complete or partial circle of stones, and port-hole stone dividing the chamber.

Historic England say that a survey in 1764 found a second chamber while and a third was noticed in 1766. A plan of the monument in the same year shows four portal stones two north and two south of the chamber's entrance.

Sadly, much of the original cairn was plundered to build the nearby road as well as construct a local house, farm and various other projects. There is past evidence of some shoring up of the site as an attempt to preserve it, but for sure this is a cairn that needs preserving as the years progress.

Details:

The Bridestones are located off Dial Lane, at approximately CW12 3QJ. It is best to leave Congleton on the A527 towards Biddulph and turn left for Leek at the crossroads. The chamber is around 2 miles on from here, near some trees.

The Bridestones Neolithic chambered cairn. (Andrew J. Billington/Shutterstock)

34. Congleton

'Beartown', as it is known locally, is a great base for exploring all parts of the county.

Mentioned as 'Cogeltone' in the Domesday Book, it was under the ownership of the Earl of Chester after William the Conqueror gifted his nephew the land. The earl fortified it and built its castle in 1208. More than 200 years later, in 1451, widespread flooding of the River Dane forced the town to be practically rebuilt on higher ground.

The reference to the bear comes from the fact Congleton was well known for its cockfights and bear-baiting in the 1600s. On one occasion, the town's famous bear died just before the Congleton Wakes and knowing what a draw it was, the decision was taken to use money being saved for a replacement bible on a new animal instead. The thought was that the funds raised at the annual festivities would pay back the loan. However, as so often happens with local legends, the story now states that the bible was sold to raise funds for the bear...

Today, many small businesses ply their trade in a fairly archetypical town centre. Almost opposite the town hall is the superb Ye Olde White Lion public house, which was built in the sixteenth to seventeenth century, while the Lion & Swan, on Swan Bank, has that historical charm too.

From here you can stroll to Lawton Street and see the bath house and garden. It is thought that it was built by William Lowndes in the 1820s.

Details:
Congleton is easy to locate take J17, the A534, from the M6. For details on the bath house visit https://congletonbpt.wordpress.com.

35. Little Moreton Hall

The attraction of this iconic Tudor house needs no introduction. Its black and white frame looks almost ramshackle, but it was built between 1504 and 1508 to make a big impression. The original house, constructed for William Moreton, included such rooms as the Great Hall, chapel and the withdrawing room. In 1546 his son, William, replaced the west wing with a new range and fourteen years later came a new floor in the Great Hall. The south wing was added by 1562 and included a third storey and long gallery.

The hall remained with the Moreton family until 1938 when the National Trust took ownership. Understandably, looking after a Grade I listed building of such a design and a Scheduled Ancient Monument is a big task and a series of restorations and works have taken place to ensure it maintains its structural integrity and stay open to visitors. In late 2018, it was rewired to keep up to date with fire safety regulations at a cost of £200,000.

Above left: A view along the uneven wooden floor and wall panels in the long gallery. (National Trust Images/Andreas von Einsiedel)

Above right: The fireplace in the Gallery Chamber. (National Trust Images/James Dobson)

Below: Visitors at the hall. (National Trust Images/John Millar)

Guided tours offer the best way to see the ground floor for a fuller picture – and there are costumed interpreters to help. You can also dress like a Tudor too.

Inside, there are some real gems to be found. The fireplace in the Gallery Chamber is a real draw for instance as is a walk along the long gallery.

Details:

The house is open to the public from April to December each year. It can be found at from junction 17 of the M6 by following the signs for Congleton. www.nationaltrust. org.uk/little-moreton-hall.

36. Sandbach Crosses

These two columns depicting several biblical scenes dominate the market square in Sandbach.

They date from the ninth century and likely note the town as the centre of a large early Saxon parish that may have also been linked to the Bishops of Lichfield.

The two crosses were originally brightly painted and adorned with jewels and metalwork to symbolise the importance of the church. There's motifs and techniques of metalworking and jewellery as well as references to Scottish and Continental art too.

They were moved to this site in the sixteenth century before being broken up a century later and cast around the area. They were then re-erected by local historian

They've been moved around and broken, but these ninth-century crosses are pride of place in the marketplace.

Dr George Ormerod in 1816. Interpretation notes exist all around the crosses and they give information on each section.

Details:
The crosses can be found in the Market Square, Sandbach, Cheshire, CW11 1AT.

37. Sandbach

Sandbach has been a market town since 1579 after Sir John Radclyffe of Ordsall was granted a royal charter by Elizabeth I.

It still holds a large Thursday market every week on Scotch Common, the High Street and in the Market Square while there is also an Indoor Market, on the ground floor of the Town Hall, open Thursdays, Fridays and Saturdays. A Farmers' and Artisan Market also appears on the second Saturday of each month from February to December.

Sandbach was mentioned in the Domesday Book as being the property of large landowner 'Bigot', with the remainder belonging to the Earl of Chester. It had a church too and was part of the Diocese of Lichfield. Even before this period, a Roman road from Middlewich to Chesterton ran through it.

Over the years it was noted for the 'production of fine worsted yarns and malt liquor,' and from the 1820s it became a focal point as a coaching stop with local inns doing a roaring trade. Therefore, it's unsurprising that there are three fantastic pubs in Sandbach!

The historic marketplace.

The first is Ye Olde Black Beare Inn, which is located beside the Market Square on the High Street. It was built in 1634 and takes its name from the area in which bear-baiting took place. It is a black and white building with thatched roof, formerly owned by Lord Crewe.

The Lower Chequer Inn is near the Market Square, on Crown Bank, and is likely to be the oldest building in the town. It dates back to 1570 with its name said to come from the 'chequered board' that was used to help educate customers to count their money. It is also believed that the old landlords were moneylenders to the locals. An ancient horseshoe is nailed to the bar and that again symbolises how important a coaching inn it was. It also used to be called the Church Inn after worshipers at St Mary's, just 50 yards away, would pop in after they had been to the service.

Across the road and a little further down the High Street is the impressive old hall that was built in 1656 by John Radclyffe, the son of Sir John. It was constructed on the site of a previous thirteenth-century manor, home of the Sondbache family, but evidence suggests that a building could have been here even earlier. In 1841, it was split, with one side becoming the rectory of Revd William Sylvester and the other becoming a pub called the Three Tuns Inn. Later, it was extended again by Lord Crewe who added a carriage arch built on the right wing.

It fell into disrepair in the twenty-first century but a campaign by the Sandbach Old Hall Action Group saw pub company Brunning & Price buy it in 2010 and undertake significant restoration. It includes two Jacobean fireplaces, one of which has a concealed priest's hole.

Details:
Sandbach is off junction 17 of the M6.

38. Nantwich

Nantwich is a bijou place with antique shops and other boutiques mixing with well-known chain stores.

There is evidence of Roman activity in the region with the area's salt being used as a preservative. In the Domesday Book it is recorded to have eight salt houses and castle, as well as being one of the seven Hundreds of Cheshire. Later, it was burned to the ground by the Normans.

Another fire destroyed most of the town in 1583, with 'Churche's Mansion' one of only a few to survive. This is a stunning black and white timber building located on the way into the town centre; it's worth parking near the church and walking back along Hospital Street to visit.

It was built in 1577 by Thomas Cleese, a carpenter who also worked at Little Moreton Hall for Richarde Churche and his wife Margerye. The Churche's were wealthy merchants who bought property on this street as well as other estates in Cheshire and Shropshire.

Black-and-white panelled buildings in the town centre, Nantwich.

By 1930, the mansion had been in the family for more than 350 years and it was sold to Dr Edgar Myott, who bought it to save it from demolition. There was a rumour that it would be dismantled and reassembled in the United States. His son Richard continued the restoration before it became home of Adams Antiques until 2018. At the time of writing it had been sold with plans to re-establish it as a specialist fish restaurant.

What the new owners will get is a superb building that retains its wonderful eye-catching features, and that is down to the work of the Myotts and Adams Antiques. It has oak panelling alongside gilt carved heads and figures and immaculate gardens.

When fire wiped out much of Nantwich, Queen Elizabeth contributed heavily to the town's rebuilding, showing its importance as probably the second most influential place in Cheshire outside Chester.

Archetypical black and white framed buildings are dotted around the town centre and it hosts a traditional market at the junction of Market Street and Churchyardside every Tuesday, Thursday and Saturday, while St Mary's Church cuts a fine sight at any time of the year with its lit frontage – particularly at Remembrance Day and in the festive season.

Details:
Nantwich is best visited via the A500 from junction 16 of the M6. There is plenty of parking available and the car park off Hospital Road, near St Mary's, is a great option.

Churche's Mansion just outside the main centre.

South West

39. Hack Green

Sometimes a gem stays with you for a long time. I've been fascinated with the history of the Cold War and particularly the aftermath of an attack ever since I discovered a Royal Observer Corps Post while researching another of the *50 Gems* series. It opened up a whole new area of underground discoveries for this speleologist and reflection of the world I was growing up in when I was a lot younger.

Visiting Hack Green Secret Nuclear Bunker married those two interests together and brought with it a sense of poignancy, empathy and terror I never expected. This was a site of preparation for a nuclear attack, an operational Cold War base, the foundation of civil defence in the region and a reminder of how far we've come since the threats of that period.

A vast array of monitoring equipment, as well as nuclear weapons.

Naturally, some will say we are closer to that than ever before; Hack Green helps you to put that into context.

The bunker's director is Lucy Siebert and we sat down in the base's NAAFI Canteen, with its cat Goulash, to find out how this sleepy corner of Cheshire became a defence hub.

'Back in 1938, the air ministry saw that war with Germany was looming, so they picked a number of strategic sites to build facsimiles,' Lucy tells me.

Here, they built a replica of Crewe railway station with the aim that when the Luftwaffe came over, they would blow this up instead of Crewe.

In the early days of the war it was too dangerous to fly during the day so the only way they could navigate blackout Britain was by the moon glinting off the railway tracks. Therefore, they found the real rail exchanges and Operation Starfish was a bit of a failure.

Then, we became a Chain Home Radar Station and by the end of the Second World War 650 airmen and women were working here, spotting bombers. In 1953, they built a ROTOR bunker here. It was the largest radar operation ever committed to and close to 15 per cent of the net wealth of the nation was invested. The plan was to have 2,500 radar stations that would protect the upper airspace of Britain against Soviet nuclear bombers.

It did that successfully for about 80 days before they turned it off. It had taken so much time and effort to commission it that the Russians had developed Intercontinental Ballistic Missiles and ROTOR couldn't spot them.

In the early '60s, we became Mersey Radar North, policing civilian and military aircraft in the skies as well as spotting any Soviet bombers that went past. In 1963, all responsibilities for that were transferred to RAF Lindholme and we were put on a care and maintenance basis. That is what we did for a long time until 1979, when Margaret Thatcher's government decided to significantly beef up the offence and defence of Britain.

Twelve Regional Government Headquarters (RGHQ) were established and we were named as 10:2. We were created to protect the bureaucratic integrity of government in the event of an attack. We did that here until 1992, when we

The A.W.D.R.E.Y detected nuclear explosions.

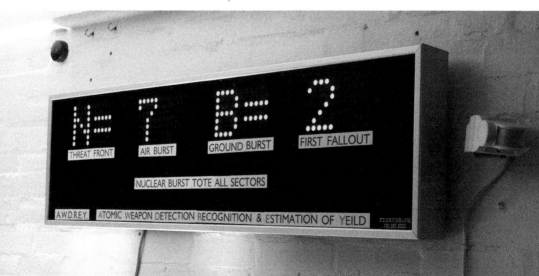

The Ballistic Missile Early Warning System (BMEWS) room.

were closed because the threat had diminished, and it was costing £4.2 million a year to keep us running.

Declassified in 1993, it lay dormant and empty until Rodney Siebert and his family took over ownership.

'My family came here in 1996,' Lucy continues.

My dad always fancied a bunker so when I was 6 years old he asked if I wanted to move to Cheshire and own a bunker. I said yes and here we are! After a couple of months my mum Angela said we should open it as a museum, and it took about a year to get enough of a collection together.

My mum and dad are still here but I have been running it for the last 7 or so years; it is a different family business for sure but one which is quite normal for me. I was born on the day the Berlin Wall came down and now I am running a Cold War museum.

Here, you get to experience what life would have been like in an active Cold War base. Lots of people don't know what to expect from a bunker and probably think it is an empty concrete hole in the ground. But it is full of equipment and full of what they would have needed to survive and prepare the nation.

Historically, the gravity of what we really are surprises people. In the event of a national emergency or something that would have taken down a significant portion of the population, we would have made sure that people survived and continued to survive.

If you came through the attack, the work here would have meant you survived for three months, six months, a year, two years and beyond. It was really important. Civil defence is often misunderstood and misrepresented, but the work done here still informs the preparations we have today.

Home Office briefings would have happened in here.

I realise this comes across like heavy stuff and it certainly is in parts. There are plenty of displays that bring the stark reality of nuclear war up close and personal. But it's fun too … seriously.

'Kids can learn and interact with real equipment,' Lucy adds. 'We have the real stuff and in today's day and age, kids don't get to play on that sort of thing. They can do it here and be in an environment which is completely historic. I would say it is an experience rather than a museum; you can experience the Cold War and the threat, alongside the excitement of being in a secret underground base.'

I don't want to spoil the experience, but I would say that the nuclear shelter and the Ballistic Missile Early Warning System (BMEWS) room, where you can press a button to simulate a real attack scenario, are by far and away the scariest and most brilliant things I have experienced when writing any of my *50 Gems*.

Starting in the canteen, you follow the numbers around the base and get to see what life would have been like at Hack Green. Your tour includes where nuclear fallout would have been tracked by top scientists, communications and BBC broadcast centres, Home Office briefing and conference rooms and their still operational radio equipment, a ROC Post, bunk rooms, the actual equipment Thatcher used to signal the attacking of the Belgrano in the Falklands conflict and a whole lot more.

It is incredible, stark, frightening and weirdly reassuring. The fact that the government had all this in place in the event of an attack, to make sure survivors had the best chance of living, is pretty sobering. Lucy and the team at Hack Green have created something that is educational and entertaining, non-political and utterly fascinating.

There's also a theatre to watch the banned BBC documentary *The War Game*, see wall displays of various bits of information about nuclear attacks, shelters and read the wonderful Cold War Tales section.

Lucy says:

We have nuclear weapons on display here – generations of our nuclear defence – and you can come and look at it in the eyeballs. The repercussions of what would have happened are here too. People can see that as a political thing, but that's not the case here. We present the actualities of what it is like and that is why the defence element is so poignant. People think of nuclear war as 'attack', but they don't think about how we prepared for the long haul after that.

It is important to understand what nuclear warfare and defence looks like alongside emergency planning. Nuclear war is very misrepresented in the media; what people think it is like and what it does to society is very different from the way it is portrayed.

We have a collection of Cold War stories that are worth pausing to look at. Some are dark and some are funny but there is a lot of fear also. So much was kept secret during that period – people didn't talk about it, they just collected extra cans at home. It was a war that was run on a personal level.

Coming here, seeing it, living it and exploring it, gives you a sense of what was happening at the time. You wouldn't create a centre like this unless the threat was very real – the government just doesn't commit millions of pounds if they didn't think it was necessary. The bunker here cost more than £32 million.

Bringing the story of Hack Green to the 30,000 visitors it welcomes each year isn't just confined to the tour. Writing workshops, radioactivity sessions, ghost hunts and re-enactments take place all-year round. It is all weather attraction you can spend all day at. It is a way for people to put a context on the everyday and understand something that is big, political and different.

Of course, the bunker isn't a 'secret' anymore, but I had to ask: are there areas of it that still remain under lock and key?

Lucy concludes with a smile, 'Yes, there are places the public aren't allowed to see. There are some bits that aren't accessible because they are in use. It's a secret bunker after all!'

Details:

Hack Green Secret Nuclear Bunker, French Lane, Nantwich, CW5 8AL, is situated just off the A530 Whitchurch Road, a few miles outside Nantwich. Take junction 16 of the M6 motorway and follow the signs to Nantwich, then Whitchurch on the A530. www.hackgreen.co.uk.

Grab your rations in the canteen.

40. Marbury

Marbury is a small but charming village located in the parish of Marbury cum Quoisley.

It is thought to have been settled since Saxon times, as it was recalled as 'Merberie' in the Domesday Book, but evidence suggests it could have seen activity as early as the Bronze Age. Today, it features some real gems including St Michael's Church, which overlooks Marbury Big Mere.

While a church was on the site at the end of the thirteenth century, this building dates from 200 years hence. It underwent significant restoration at the end of the nineteenth century. At its exterior are several carvings of flora and fauna but also some gargoyles including monkeys and 'ugly' faces.

Marbury village, which means 'the burg by a lake', is just as fascinating too. On the village green is an oak tree planted to commemorate the Battle of Waterloo in 1815, while there are some outstanding sixteenth and seventeenth century black and white cottages. The renovated Swan dates from 1765.

The Big Mere is an important wildlife habitat and around 500 metres in length. It is a private fishing lake but does attract several species as do the nearby Quoisley Meres, which are SSSIs. These smaller 'lakes' are Wetlands of International Importance and part of the Midland Meres and Mosses RAMSAR site. In particular the reed beds support more than 100 plant species.

Details:
Marbury can be found off the A49 by following Marbury Road.

41. Malpas

Its name may derive from the Old French for 'bad passage' or 'bad way' but there is little to be concerned about when visiting Malpas.

The moniker is thought to refer to the wildness of its location and the fact it was vulnerable to Welsh raids. It's right on the border between Shropshire and Wales but is, of course, in the county of Cheshire.

Malpas certainly existed in 1121 but the Domesday Book recorded a settlement of 'Depenbech' in this area at the end of the eleventh century, which belonged to the Baron of Malpas, Robert FitzHugh. He received land on the border because of his role in defending the area from raids. It was protected by a motte-and-bailey castle, evidence of which is still visible behind the church, although it is difficult to gain access to the actual site. In 1281, it was awarded a charter for a market and fair.

The town retains that medieval street pattern as well as several features from his past. The Red Lion pub dates from the seventeenth century and was also a well-known stop for coaches on routes between Chester, Shrewsbury, Birmingham

St Oswald's
Church is well
worth a visit!

and London during the eighteenth and nineteenth centuries. The market cross is an obvious meeting point, but the medieval version was removed around 200 years ago. The present structure was erected in 1877 as a memorial to a former Malpas rector. The iron dome at its base also had a valve for piped water. Then there's the Wigfield Terrace, built in 1854 by the Rev Henry Winfield as six almshouses for the poor.

The real hub of the town is St Oswald's Church, which is up the hill from the cross. It was built in the fourteenth century, likely on the site of a private chapel for the castle. It has a medieval painting and gilded ceiling that is just lovely, a funeral hatchment above the nave, an impressive Lewis organ, Flemish window panels and a thirteenth-century oak chest. It also contains a fifteenth-century eight-sided stone font and stalls with carved misericords.

Details:
Malpas can be found off the A41 to the south of Cheshire. It is well signposted and there are some interpretation boards around the town that will guide you to the best historical sites.

42. Holt Castle

Holt Castle was built in around 1282 by John De Warenne, the Earl of Surrey, after he was granted the area following Edward I's final defeat of the Welsh. It had an unusual pentagonal design and briefly served as the treasure house for Richard II before becoming the principle home of Sir William Stanley at the end of the fifteenth century. He played a pivotal role in the demise of Richard III at Bosworth Field.

Sadly, the site was used as a stone quarry by Thomas Grosvenor in 1675 to build Samwell Hall, a predecessor of the current Eaton Hall. As a result, very little survives apart from the central courtyard.

The project to conserve this Scheduled Ancient Monument took place between 2012 and 2014 and was funded by a Rural Development Grant and by Cadw.

The work removed vegetation, reconsolidated the masonry and created interpretation boards. They've done a fine job too.

Details:
Holt Castle is an open access site. A footpath leads from Castle Street via Castle Gardens (LL13 9AX) to the castle site. Parking and toilets are available at LL13 9JF.

Above and below: The remnants of Holt Castle. (Steve Grenter/Wrexham Council)

43. Beeston Castle

Beeston Castle is an impressive ruin set on a crag beside 40 acres of woodland.

It is a location with a history much deeper than when it was built in the 1220s by Ranulf, 6th Earl of Chester. Tools from the Neolithic period have been found in the area as well as 'burial mounds and funerary material' from the Bronze Age. There is also evidence of defences dating to the Iron Age when the existing bank was enlarged by a large ditch to create a hill fort.

Ranulf was a keen supporter of King John and received titles and acreage for his loyalty. After fighting in the Crusades, he returned to find land being confiscated by the then Henry III's judiciary – and he therefore bolstered his political status by building at Beeston. The gatehouses and tower are likely to date from this time.

Henry III took ownership of the castle from John le Scot, Ranulf's nephew, in 1237, and it remained in royal ownership until the sixteenth century. It withstood a long siege in 1644–45 but was surrendered by the Royalists after the Battle of Rowton in 1645 and partially demolished.

From there, it was passed to Sir Thomas Mostyn in the late seventeenth century before being extensively quarried in the eighteenth, which saw the outer gatehouse partly removed.

English Heritage took over the castle in 1984 and it remains a tremendous asset to the organisation who manage the site superbly.

Details:
Beeston Castle is around 11 miles south of Chester, off the A49. Parking is available nearby for £3. The best postcode for navigation is CW6 9TX. www.english-heritage. org.uk/visit/places/beeston-castle-and-woodland-park/.

Exterior view of the battlements and well of the inner bailey at Beeston Castle. (Historic England Archive)

44. Hatchmere

Hatchmere is a beautiful and tranquil lake located next to The Carriers Inn, less than a mile from Delamere Forest.

It is a part of a nature reserve overseen by the Chester Wildlife Trust (CWT), is an SSSI and was formed when glacial drift deposited water after the last ice age.

What's impressive about the mere and its 31-acre reserve is the many birds that visit and the expansive and different types of vegetation on its shores. You can enjoy this on a simple and straightforward circuit, which is around 1.5 miles long.

You can see great crested grebe, reed bunting and willow warbler here as well as up to thirteen species of dragonfly and damselfly according to the CWT. It's also possible to link up your walk with Delamere Forest, which is right on the doorstep.

Hatchmere is a haven for wild swimmers, with a designated and marked area for those who fancy a dip. Try it … it's bracing!

Next to the lake is The Carriers Inn, which dates back to 1637. It was originally a smithy.

Details:
The mere can be accessed from Delamere Road (WA6 6NY). For wild swimming information visit www.hatchmere.com.

Hatchmere is an SSSI...

...and a great swimming spot.

45. Delamere Forest

Once part of the great forests of Mara and Mondrem, Delamere is the county's largest area of woodland. It covers around 2,400 acres and contains a mixture of deciduous and evergreen trees alongside Blakemere Moss, which is just over half a mile in length.

The lake is a centrepiece that's impossible to avoid as you walk through the forest. It attracts hundreds of black-headed gulls and they light up the water with a clamour of noise and clatter.

It was drained at the beginning of the nineteenth century but a scheme to plant oak and Scots pine in its place was unsuccessful. In 1998, clear felling took place and it was refilled. The nearby Norley and Blains Mosses – important peatlands – have also been recently restored. These hollows formed during the last Ice Age as the sheet melted. They were filled with peat but over the last 200 years or so have been drained and hidden by trees. This vegetation has now been removed to allow the mosses to refill and help wetland plants thrive.

Also, in the south-west corner of Delamere is Black Lake – a 'quaking bog' or a schwingmoor – that is also an SSSI. It forms when sphagnum moss and cotton grass, as well as other plants, create a 'raft' that then floats on the water. It is a popular area for bog flora and dragonflies too and is managed by the Cheshire Wildlife Trust.

The overall conservation of Delamere fell into the remit of the Forestry Commission in 1924. Firstly, they managed it for timber production, but it's the recreational and environmental value of the forest that is now key to its attraction.

Blakemere Moss.

Above and below: Delemere is full of gems.

Details:
Delamere Forest can be found at CW8 2HZ. There are four official car parks – the Forest Centre car park, the Treetops car park, which is close to Delamere train station, Old Pale car park – a short way beyond Forest Centre car park and a start point for all the trails – and the Whitefield car park, the most suitable site for large vehicles. www.forestryengland.uk/delamere-forest.

46. Chester Zoo

Chester Zoo is an incredible place of conservation whose reach stretches far beyond its 125 acres. Its strategic objective is to prevent extinction of the world's valuable species and eco-diversity by achieving the greatest conservation impact, providing exceptional animal and plant care and by being a world-class visitor attraction.

It's certainly that, being probably the most varied zoo in the country with a spellbinding experience that not only leaves you in awe of the fauna of our world but empowered to help protect it for future generations. It is a place of learning; you can see endangered species up close and witness how the zoo's award-winning projects provide best practice and support for conservation all over the world.

The Islands at Chester Zoo. (Chester Zoo)

Rhinoceros Hornbill. (Chester Zoo)

Therefore, it's all the more remarkable that it was founded by just one person. George Mottershead was an animal lover who had 'a dream of a zoo with no bars' after he visited Belle Vue in Manchester. He was a little eccentric and a maverick in his approach – he needed to be – but ultimately, he was a determined chap who just wouldn't give up. In 1930, with a family and a small group of animals, he bought Oakfield Manor, a ramshackle house in Upton, on the outskirts of Chester, and 7 acres of land for £3,500. A year later it opened as zoo, and in 1934 the North of England Zoological Society was born, establishing his venture and its aims as a charity.

His energy to create something special and unique earned him an OBE, an honorary Master of Science degree and a term as president of the International Union of Zoo Directors. He died in 1978, aged eight-four.

George's vision and original zoo is now nothing short of phenomenal. 7 acres have become 125, and there are more than 21,000 animals from around 500 different species on the site. His charity also supports projects from around the world and through its wildlife conservation campaign, Act for Wildlife, is helping to save highly threatened species from extinction.

Chester Zoo has more than eighty different projects across thirty different countries. The zoo is ever expanding with new grassland, forest, foothill and floodplain attractions to accompany the relatively recent Islands – all designed to bring people closer to wildlife.

Details:
Chester Zoo can be found off junction 15 of the M56. Follow the brown sides from the A41. For prices and opening times visit www.chesterzoo.org.

Below left: Warty pigs. (Chester Zoo)

Below right: Happy times in the Islands! (Chester Zoo)

Sumatran tiger.
(Chester Zoo)

47. Chester Cathedral

Chester Cathedral stands proud in Chester but within its confines you wouldn't know a bustling city centre lies just metres from its walls.

It stands on the site of an original Saxon church dedicated to St Werburgh and in 1092 was re-founded as a Benedictine abbey by Hugh Lupus, Earl of Chester. Evidence of that Norman and Romanesque structure can be seen in the north transept and a series of Gothic rebuilding programmes from 1250, and a major Victorian restoration, resulted in the building you see today.

A tour is the best way to discover the cathedral and I was lucky enough to be guided by Nick Fry, bedesman at the cathedral, whose passion and extraordinary knowledge of the site is second to none.

'Chester Cathedral was never intended to be a cathedral,' he opened. 'It was built as a monastery and that ended with the Dissolution of the Monasteries by Henry VIII in 1540. Less than a year later, it became the Cathedral of the Diocese of Chester and the same staff carried through. As a result, nothing happened here in terms of damage or destruction. Therefore, what you see here is not a purpose-built medieval cathedral, but one of the best examples in the country of a monastic complex. The cloisters and the quire are from the medieval church and they are spectacular.'

Our route around the cathedral first visits the Consistory Court, which is the only one of its type remaining in the country. Nick says it was an ecclesiastical court through the sixteenth to nineteenth centuries and had legal responsibility for cases such as heresy, martial disputes, slander, libel, non-attendance at church and so forth.

Above: The cathedral is inspiring.

Below: The Chester Imp.

Back in the main part of the cathedral, Nick begins to point out some of its treasures, and there are so many to find. High up on the left-hand side in the gallery is a carving of a Chester imp – a devil in chains.

'The story says that a monk was walking down the gallery here and saw the devil looking through the window,' he explains.

He reported this to the abbot who told him to put up a carving of the devil in chains to scare the evil spirits away.

But if you were to define a true treasure of the building then it would be the Quire. All the wood carving dates from 1380 and it is said to be the finest of its type in the country. It was completed by the King's Master Carpenters and was the best money could buy which is why the quality is so exceptional.

Look at the style too. It isn't the style of a provincial church but the style of the Royal Court in London. This is why it is so significant, but they had a practical use too. They were carved to keep the draft off the back of the monks' necks and that would be welcome relief as they would spend most of their day here.

Then you have the ledges on the seats. Monks could sit for a couple of minutes but the rest of the time they had to stand. Those ledges meant they could sit … but with their heavy robes on it would look like they were standing.

The seats are misericords, from the Latin misericordia, which means pity … out of pity for the monks' legs. Each one has its own symbolic story to tell. On one are two herons; the Disciples were fishers of man and herons are fishers too.

If you had to pick out one particular carving it would be the elephant and castle. The story says that the image came over with the Crusaders who fought on the back of elephants. Whoever carved it certainly hadn't seen an elephant in 1380 so when they did the feet and legs, the only four-legged big animal they knew was a horse and hence this is what you have depicted. It represents the church carrying the world on its back.

We continue the tour and come to the medieval shrine of St Werburgh, who is the patron saint of Chester. Nick says that relics were brought to this site to save them

The quire.

from the Vikings and people would make the pilgrimage to see them. St Werburgh died in 706 but the present shrine dates from around 1530.

'There are only seven shrines like this in the country,' he adds. 'The relics went in the top and the pilgrims sat around the bottom. It was dismantled by Henry VIII and wasn't put back until the nineteenth century. Apparently, the relics are reburied here.'

Chester Cathedral is a varied and fascinating place. We walk past the various memorials, the painting on a silk web, the nineteenth-century organ, which has nearly 5,000 pipes and eventually into the cloisters. This is where the monks lived and wrote their manuscripts. The stained glass here dates from the 1920s and '30s, which means there was nothing but fresh air around the monks in medieval times.

In the centre of the cathedral is the monastery's fish pond – fish being central to their diet and symbolic – while the statue of the woman at the Well was created by Steven Broadbent in 1992. Returning inside and further around the cloisters is a door, which was the monks' only real link with the outside world. It has a carving on the left of a drum and on the right, bagpipes. The symbolism? Through that door was noise.

There was certainly a lot of 'din' from the last room on our tour – the refectory. This was the monks' dining room; the abbot would be sat up on a raised platform

Below left: The cloisters would have been a cold place for monks to write their scriptures.

Below right: The fish pond and sculpture are a great place to reflect.

with guests on either side while others would be at long tables in front. They would offer hospitality to pilgrims who would visit the shrine.

Nick said:

This is an exceptional room. It is a survivor of the medieval period and we are lucky we can use it as our refectory now. Meals would be taken in silence and the monks would read out a chapter from the Bible.

The reason this room has survived is because it was used as a school when the monastery was dissolved. It was the Kings School which is now outside Chester. You can see the school kids carving their names in walls.

It's so obvious that I can't believe they didn't have permission to do that.

Details:
Chester Cathedral is open to visitors on Monday to Saturday from 9 a.m. to 6 p.m. and Sunday from 1 p.m. to 4 p.m. www.chestercathedral.com.

48. Chester Rows

Chester is a historic city with many fascinating features and quirks. Although it has changed somewhat over the years with its retail offering, the Rows have remained an iconic place for businesses to ply their trade in a special setting. Some have enhanced their surroundings – expanding outwards and onto to the rows – while others have altered their frontage to keep in with the heritage.

To put it into simple terms, the Rows are 'continuous half-timbered galleries' reached by steps from ground level. They form a second row above the streets along Watergate Street, Northgate Street, Eastgate Street and Bridge Street in the city centre. There's nothing like them anywhere in the world.

The first written record of their existence came at the end of the thirteenth century and dating has confirmed this timescale in some of the structures. Some of the original buildings, including the Three Old Arches in Bridge Street, which could be the oldest shopfront in the country, still survive. There are also stone undercrofts beneath; around twenty remain and we discover one in gem 50. There is one on Eastgate – Brown's Crypt, which dates from 1290 – and three on Watergate Street at Nos 11, 21 and 37.

There are several theories at how the Rows came to be. One suggests that following a fire in 1278 an extra row was built to improve the commercial potential of businesses. Development had to occur vertically because of the restricted space around the city. The Rows could have been built on old Roman remains also, the new structures making best use of what was available.

Defoe says it was to keep folk dry in inclement weather and there is also a suggestion that they could have been a security aid – in case of burglary you could trap would be robbers for justice to prevail!

Above and below: The Rows.

Details:
Chester is well signposted off the M56. Parking is available all around the city and there is a park and ride scheme.

49. Chester Walls

Chester's environs are probably the most well known in the whole of Cheshire and the North West.

Deva, as it was called in Roman times, was founded as a fortress in the first century AD. What is special about this city is the evidence of that occupation, from the amphitheatre and gardens to the red sandstone walls which enclose it, is largely retained.

Chester is the only place in the country that still has its complete circuit of walls and therefore a walk around them, close to 2 miles in length, is a must.

It is thought that work on these defensive structures began around AD 70–80. They were originally constructed of earth and turf with a basic wooden stake fence or palisade. Twenty years later local red sandstone was used to fortify them, and it likely took another century before they were complete.

Following the Norman Conquest, these defences were extended to the west and south – the circuit complete – and they were further strengthened before the Civil War.

This iconic clock celebrates Queen Victoria's diamond jubilee.

Above: The River Dee.

Right: The walls stretch for nearly 2 miles around the city.

Access to them can be taken in a number of ways but is best via four main gateways – Bridgegate, Eastgate, Watergate and Northgate. It is worth nothing that the walls are constantly being maintained due to their sandstone construction and the steps near Northgate, at the time of writing, were being stabilised and therefore closed to the public. Work to repair them began in 2016, but contractors found important archaeology in the process. They unearthed a complex structure of towers, a gaol and a medieval dungeon.

Eastgate has, for 2,000, years, been the main entrance to the city. It is now Georgian but still a busy access point. It was here that Henry IV displayed the remains of Henry 'Hotspur' Percy as a warning to other traitors. The severed heads of Sir Richard Venables and Sir Richard Vernon were also put on show. The iconic clock was added to celebrate Queen Victoria's diamond jubilee.

Next is Newgate. An access point was recorded here as Wolfeld's Gate in the late twelfth century but could have originated before 1066. It later became Peppergate. The gateway was rebuilt in 1768 and then became the neo-Gothic one it is today in 1938.

Further on you come to the River Dee and Bridgegate, which guarded the entrance from the Old Dee Bridge that was built in 1387. This was the route into the city from Wales. The English side of the river was protected by Bridgegate and a fortified round tower while on the other side there was an outer gateway complete with drawbridge and portcullis. Here, you can also see a Norman weir in the water, which is from around 1092.

Watergate was the site of a busy port. The River Dee deep enough for ships to offload at the city long before it silted. The tower was built to defend this important access point.

Finally, two other interesting places on the walls are Pemberton's parlour, named after an eighteenth-century 'murenger' who was responsible for the upkeep of the walks and the King Charles Tower.

The former is a decorative alcove constructed on the remains of a medieval round tower while the latter was a medieval watch tower. It fell into disrepair and so the city's guilds leased it with the proviso that they kept it in good order. This structure later become the Phoenix Tower after the emblem of the Painters' Company that met here.

It is thought that King Charles stood here on 24 September 1645 as he watched his army being defeated at the Battle of Rowton Heath.

Details:
Access to the walls is available all around the circuit but it is best to start at one of the gates mentioned above. Newgate is a good place to begin the walk as you can visit the Roman amphitheatre and gardens too.

50. The Falcon Inn

It seems inevitable that our tour of Cheshire gems would finish in a pub ... and I make no apologies for completing the trip with probably the best inn I have visited.

The Falcon is a Grade II listed building that has been in place for nearly 840 years. What survives now is only half of the medieval townhouse that was constructed at the back end of the twelfth century. It would have had a huge hall that ran parallel to the street.

The Falcon is a great venue for a drink with an interesting history.

The cellar is an undercroft that contains timber beams from the thirteenth century while stone piers from the same period can be seen in the front bar. Two other timbers date from 1200.

I visited the Falcon after concluding my tour of Chester and naturally asked the barman for a pint. He served it up and we got talking about the inn's history.

'Do you want to see the cellar?' he said.

I nodded and within sixty seconds I was in the undercroft seeing those timber beams as well as a Roman safe and smugglers cupboard that would have dropped down to the river below.

Jamie told me that the inn was originally a townhouse that was altered by Sir Richard Grosvenor, a leading Royalist, in 1643. The row was enclosed and that set

Apparently, this is a Roman safe...

The bar.

the precedent for other buildings to do the same. Between 1778 and 1878 it was a licensed inn but by 1879 it had become a temperance house.

Having a pint in the Falcon feels like you're being transported back to those early days. Little has changed from the sixteenth- and seventeenth-century renovation. It feels old and atmospheric.

The Falcon was virtually derelict by the 1970s before the Grosvenor estate donated it to the Falcon Trust, who reopened it in 1992.

'We have three ghosts here too,' Jamie adds as I order my second beer. 'There's a young boy in cellar I have spoken to. It's a great place to work with lots of character.'

I'll drink to that…

Details:
The Falcon Inn can be found on Lower Bridge Street in Chester.